JESUS' PLAN FOR A NEW WORLD

Richard Rohr, O.F.M.
with John Bookser Feister

JESUS' PLAN FOR A NEW WORLD

The Sermon on the Mount

ST. ANTHONY MESSENGER PRESS

Cincinnati, Ohio

Cover photograph ©Ewing Galloway
Cover and book design by Mary Alfieri
Diagram designs by Sandra Digman

ISBN 0-86716-203-1

Published by St. Anthony Messenger Press
Printed in the U.S.A.

DEDICATION

To my sisters, Carol and Alana,
and my brother, Tim, who have always kept
the home fires burning and supported me
in kindling other fires.

—Richard Rohr, O.F.M.

To Cathy, faithful witness to the Beatitudes.
Also to Les Schmidt, Evelyn Dettling, O.S.B.,
and the folks at Connective Ministries,
who struggle so that those who are poor
can preach good news to the rest.

—John Bookser Feister

ACKNOWLEDGMENTS

I would like to thank my confreres and friends at St. Anthony Messenger Press, who have continued to trust and support my attempts to communicate the gospel. Special thanks to John Bookser Feister who has the love, patience—and humility—to sift through my erroneous grammar and errant thoughts.

—Richard

I would like to thank the Sisters of Divine Providence of Melbourne, Kentucky, for constant inspiration. I also wish to thank my wife, Cathy, and our children, Jesse, Scott and Johnny, for their loving patience and generosity. Finally, thanks to Richard, a willing servant of the gospel.

—John

Contents

We know everything today
And believe almost nothing.

It is not reason that drives our lives,
But passion or the search for it.
It is not words and concepts,
But living images that grab our souls.
It is not what we know that haunts us at the end,
But what we did not know and don't know yet.

We must make friends with the unknowing,
What you know is just ten thousand different
    things.

But what you believe
Is what you pay attention to,
What you care about,
What finally lives and matters in you.

What you believe is not one of ten thousand things,
It is that which sees ten thousand things.

It is not what you know that matters,
Or changes anything:
It is what you believe—

And believe all the way through.

Introduction:
How to Read the Bible

T he Bible is the most controversial book in print. It has done an immense amount of good. At the same time, it probably has caused more damage than any other book in human history. That may seem like a shocking statement from a Franciscan, Catholic priest, but if you look at history, you can see how many Christians acted in oppressive, stupid and rigid ways in the name of Jesus and the gospel. That's because they didn't really understand what Jesus was up to.

Thank God that our Church is encouraging the type of scholarship and theological study that really deals with the New Testament text as the word of God, *written in human history, at a particular time and place.* Through this scholarship, we're trying to be more honest with the Bible, rather than making it say what we want it to say, what we are culturally conditioned to need or think it to say. We are beginning to understand the social, cultural, political, economic situation in which it was first written.

Not surprisingly, we're finding that a lot of the issues in the New Testament are eternal issues. (This is of course true for the Hebrew Scriptures as well.) But we create incredible misunderstanding by reading and interpreting the text without understanding its context. By digging into the work of understanding Jesus and his times, we find the New Testament to be a far richer source of spiritual life than we could ever have imagined.

This book is about the Sermon on the Mount, considered the blueprint of the Christian life-style, pronounced by Jesus himself. But the secret to understanding the Sermon on the Mount is to understand what Jesus was about when he preached it. So this book is as much about getting ready to hear the Sermon as it is about the Sermon itself. We'll be skipping all over the Gospel According to Matthew and touching on what modern scholars are saying about Jesus' public ministry.

I intentionally chose throughout the book to say, "Jesus said." I am aware that the words in print may be from the evangelist, the memory of a community thirty or more years later or the theological construct of a faith community. But, for me, all that is precisely the *living Jesus* we need to hear. Once you're ready to hear the Sermon, it requires very little explanation. That will become clearer in the first chapters of this book.

One of the problems in reading the Bible is that most of us Christians preconceive Jesus as "the divine savior of our divine Church," which prematurely settles all the dust and struggle. Such a predisposition does not open us to enlightenment by Christ, but in fact, deadens and numbs our perception. A part of us reads the Bible in order to prove this understanding of Jesus. He's God of our saved Church, which means that our Church—and we—are right. If we are honest enough to admit that bias, we may have a chance of letting go of it for a richer understanding of the gospel.

We bring our hearts to reading the Gospels, but we must bring our heads as well. We must break through our fear that these really were *people* who were with Jesus, who formed a Church, who wrote the Gospels—people like you and me. Understanding these people and their world, I hope, will finally free the Spirit more than ever in our lives.

Every indication is that the growing phenomenon in our society will be fundamentalism. Fundamentalism refuses to listen to what the Gospel authors are really saying to their communities. It enters into a nonhistorical love affair with words—I don't know how else to describe it. The human need for clarity and certitude leads fundamentalists to use sacred writings in a mechanical, closed-ended and authoritarian manner. This invariably leaves them trapped in their own cultural moment in history, and they often totally miss the real message along with the deepest challenges and consolations of Scripture.

In the name of taking the word literally, the fundamentalist is in fact missing the literal word. Isn't that ironic? The real meaning of the text is largely missed by people who say they take it all literally. In other words, the metaphorical sense, the mythological sense, the sense of religious psychology and sacred story is in fact the *literal*, real sense—just as it is when you and I talk, write and communicate with one another.

There is an especially telling passage in Mark's Gospel where Jesus becomes angry even with his disciples, who are unable to understand his clearly metaphorical language. He tells them to watch out for the leaven of the Pharisees and the leaven of Herod. Taking him literally, they began looking quizzically at one another because they did not have any bread (see Mark 8:14-16). Is "Herod Bread" a new brand that they had not heard about?

Aware of their amazing ability to miss the point, Jesus answers with impatience and a demand that they understand his language: "Do you think I am talking about bread? You're still not using your heads, are you? You still don't get the point, do you? Are you just dense? Though you have ears, you still don't hear; though you have eyes, you still don't see!" (see Mark 8:17-19).

Jesus knows the language necessary to speak of spiritual things and insists that his disciples learn it. Religion has always needed the language of metaphor, symbol, story and analogy to point to the transcendent universe. There is actually no other way. Against conventional wisdom, such usage does not demand less of us but much more. Maybe that is why we so consistently avoid sacred story in favor of mere mechanical readings that we can limit and control.

So our goal in this book will be to delve into the language of religion and emerge with a clearer understanding of the Sermon on the Mount, the Nazarene rabbi who preached it and the Gospel writers, especially Matthew, who passed it on to us. It may feel strange to approach Scripture this way. But just as God spoke to the ancients in their moment in time, we trust that God will do the same for us. The Gospels thus lead us both to faith in the Jesus who lived in our history and to faith in the eternally risen Christ, who is still teaching and still hidden within his people.

The final and full word, therefore, is that the authority of the Bible lies not just in ancient texts but in the living Christ of history,

Church, community and your own experience confirming its truth. The mystery is "Christ among you, your hope of glory" (Colossians 1:27)—this is the *living* Bible!

Finally, I must confirm and quote my mentor Saint Paul, who said a most strange but truthful thing. He said, "Christ sent me not to baptize, but to preach the gospel; and not by means of *wisdom* [emphasis mine] of language, wise words which would make the cross of Christ pointless" (1 Corinthians 1:17). I know that I am not primarily a baptizer or a writer, although I do both, but a preacher. These written words, written because of the dedication of John Bookser Feister, are not eloquent writing, but they are, I hope, new proclamation of the power and meaning of the cross for human history. If you hear the message, I will know it was not because of a well-written text of mine, but because the cross has still not been emptied of its power to transform human history. That alone will last.

Part One

GETTING READY TO HEAR JESUS

CHAPTER ONE

Jesus' New World Order

I am told that there are three kinds of cultures today, each with its own "bottom line": political cultures based on the manipulation of power, economic cultures based on the manipulation of money, and religious cultures based on the manipulation of some theory about God. (The purely kinship-based culture is largely disappearing.) These are the directions that human culture takes whenever it is left to its own devices. All three are based on some form of violence, although it is usually denied by most participants and hidden from the superficial observer. Evil gains its power from disguise, it seems. It is precisely this darkness and death that God, in Jesus, has come to destroy.

Jesus announced, lived and inaugurated for history a new social order that is an actual alternative to each of the above—and an alternative that he said (with greater authority than Karl Marx) is *inevitable*—not inevitable by reason of scientific determinism, but by the promise and grace of God. He called it the *Reign* or *Kingdom of God*. It is the subject of his inaugural address, the majority of his parables and clearly the guiding image of his entire ministry. It was also the reason that he was killed: "It is better for one man to die for the people" (John 18:14) than to question our bottom line that is holding the whole system together. When we Christians accept that Jesus was killed for the same reasons that people have been killed in all of human history (and not because he walked around saying "I am God"), we will have turned an important corner on our Jesus quest. He was rejected, as we will see, because of his worldview much more than his God-view. Yet we know that they are intrinsically connected. This now and not-yet Reign of God is the foundation for our personal hope and our cosmic optimism, but it is also the source of our deepest alienation from the world as it is. It will leave you a stranger and nomad on this earth (see Hebrews 11:13). Our task is to learn how to live in both worlds until they become one world—at least in us.

Once this guiding vision became clear to Jesus, which seems to have happened when he was about thirty and alone in the desert, everything else came into perspective. In fact, Matthew's Gospel says "From then onwards" (4:17), Jesus began his preaching. He had his outer and absolute reference point that allowed him to judge and evaluate everything else properly. This was his Archimedian point, if you will, from which he could—and did—move the whole world. His center point was clear and unquestionable for him—which is the precise nature of faith—and that allowed him to live and teach with the same simple clarity and certitude.

This center point, however, was not an idea or a theory about anything (which differentiates it from the other three kinds of culture), but, in fact, a Person—a thoroughly reliable and even lovable person that he called his "Father." This new world order is based on the experience of a God who is experienced personally. Jesus seems to be saying that God is not a philosophical system, a theory to be proven or an energy to be discussed or controlled, although we have often reduced God to such. Jesus believes that God is a Person to be imitated, enjoyed and loved. We only seem to know God by relating to God, almost as if God refuses to be known apart from love. It is all about relationship. As Martin Buber, the Jewish philosopher mystic, put it, "All real living is meeting." That simple and totally available experience makes all the difference "in the world."

Jesus' new alternative is not just another religious culture, however. This is pivotal to understanding the unique character of his new world order. As opposed to a religious culture, which is always using God for cultural purposes of control and manipulating people through religious imagery, the Reign of God disallows both possibilities. This is the difference between True Transcendence and its disguises, between the True Sacred and what we might call the false sacred. The false sacred can be spotted because it is always self-serving and other-destroying. Anthropologist René Girard calls it "the old sacrificial system," for it uses and misuses God to sacralize the creation of victims.[1] It might be "old," but as we

4

know, we continue this universal pattern to our own day, and in ever more sophisticated ways.

It seems to begin with Cain's killing of his brother, Abel, when Cain feels unworthy and unloved by Yahweh God. We know we are dealing with a universal and archetypal pattern that continues through time when even the very first chapters of the Bible tell us that brother kills brother. The "evil" one must always be killed so that "I" can be worthy, loved and moral. Another group, nationality, class or religion has to be named wrong so that "I" can feel right.

The insecure and false self seems to need an enemy to scapegoat so that it can feel superior and saved. False gods, by definition, must be appeased. The true God needs nothing. The true God invites us into an unthinkable communion.

Ironically, a religious culture actually works to a degree and for a time. It gives individuals and groups enough sense of cohesion and solidarity to create a partial community. With our immorality cleverly denied and carried by the scapegoated person or group, we actually feel rather good about ourselves. Remember the American camaraderie for the twenty-some years following World War II? Our evil lay unrecognized on the heads of Germans, Japanese and Communists. They were the bad losers, and we were the good victors. It was true on a certain political level, but not necessarily true at all on the level that Jesus says is final and definitive. It is no surprise that many people continue to confuse a mere religious culture (read: law and order) with the much more subversive Reign of God.

The True Sacred, which is synonymous with the Reign of God, is of an entirely different order and significance. On the level of experience, the True Sacred always reveals that:

1) God is One and for all.
2) God is sovereign to any group ownership or personal manipulation.
3) God is available as free gift and not through sacrificing another.
4) God needs no victims and creates no victims.

Jesus personifies this type of God and speaks defiantly in defense of such a God. Nowhere is he more succinct than when he quotes the Prophet Hosea, "Go and learn the meaning of the words: *Mercy is what pleases me, not sacrifice*" (Matthew 9:13).

Creating Idols

When there is no experience of the True Sacred, we will always fall into the worship of the false sacred. The false sacred will invariably become a pretext and even a holy justification for prejudice, marginalization of others, scapegoating and violence. If God is not God, in other words, we will ourselves become gods and create strange gods. Why wouldn't we? If God is not God, we will also demonize others as a way of validating our fragile identity. Such a pattern has become increasingly apparent in human history. Only an entrance into the Great Compassion frees us from the need to divide our reality into the good guys and the bad guys. Or as Jesus puts it, "be children of your Father in heaven, for he causes his sun to rise on the bad as well as the good, and sends down rain to fall on the upright and the wicked alike" (Matthew 5:45).

Without a Forgiveness great enough to embrace even the dark side of things, we are burdened (and I mean burdened) with our own need to explain and to judge everything. Who is right now? Who was wrong there? These are eventual and important moral questions, but you cannot, you dare not, lead with them—without making love and compassion impossible. Thus, this is the centrality, and yet unbelievability, of Jesus' words "Do not judge" (Matthew 7:1).

The True Sacred, the Reign of God, unmasks and relativizes the false sacred. It is revolutionary in the truest sense of the term. The True Sacred desacralizes all else and yet ironically establishes the basis for the authentic holiness of everything else. It is a paradox that the modern world resists. There is no real philosophical basis for calling something holy or sacred unless we are recognizing a transcendent origin, that which is beyond our creation and our control. Once the True Sacred is honored, however, we are free and even compelled to recognize its reflection in all of its creatures and all of creation. Thus, Jesus' name for God implies not only benevolence but also source and origin: "Father." (Gender is not the emphasis, although one could say that defining healthy and true fatherhood had both the intention and the effect of subverting all patriarchy and false masculinity.)

Without the True Sacred we are all at one another's mercy and subject to one another's whimsical judgments. Under the True Sacred we are at the mercy of One-Who-Is-Mercy. No wonder Jesus gave all his life to proclaim such a monumental liberation! Humanity has been waiting for such freedom with Messianic hope. It is the only way out of our revolving hall of mirrors, our own war of all against all, and is rightly called salvation. For Jesus, God's judgment is good news for the nations—and for the individual too. How different than how most of us think about judgment.

Conversion: Theme of the New World Order

Such a new world order is so foundationally different, so transformative of perspective, that mere education or intellectual assent is inadequate for even preliminary understanding. It demands what becomes Jesus' next favorite theme—conversion—a complete turnaround of worldviews. His teaching is summarized in one line: "The time is fulfilled, and the kingdom of God is close at hand. Repent, and believe the gospel" (Mark 1:15). Conversion is not a learning as much as it is an unlearning. Conversion is an unlearning that comes like a dove descending (see Mark 1:10) once the old world order is unmasked—and the Great Lover is revealed. No wonder we had to use phrases like falling from a horse, scales falling from our eyes (see Acts 9:18) and the crowing of the cock (Luke 22:61).

One will not, of course, turn away from what seems like the only game in town (political, economic or religious) unless one has glimpsed a more attractive alternative. Jesus is a living parable, an audiovisual icon of that more attractive alternative. We cannot even imagine it, much less imitate it, unless we see one human being do it first. Jesus has forever changed human imagination, and we are now both burdened and gladdened by the new possibility. There is good news to counter the deadening bad news, but one first has to be turned away from a conventional way of seeing.

The most unsettling of his alternative wisdom, and perhaps the most consistent, is that the outcast is in the head-start position, precisely because he or she has been excluded from the false sacred system—"the only game in town." Jesus thus begins by a most incredible statement: the poor are the blessed ones! (see Matthew 5:3). Life has already freed them from the lie that the rest of us cannot see. They are potentially turned around and given a symbolic advantage in hearing the truth: "I tell you, tax collectors and prostitutes are making their way into the kingdom of God before you" (Matthew 21:31). If the system is a mess, those outside of it are at a significant advantage!

"Empathy for the victim," therefore, became the most subversive element in his teaching, although he was only building on his Jewish tradition and sympathies. This teaching was so hard to comprehend that he had to finally *image* it in the manner of his passion and death, so we would get the message. As we see in the Gospels, Mark's in particular, the disciples themselves cannot get it. Most of the Church is still in the early stages of comprehension. Why would the "first be last" (one of his most common one-liners) unless there is something essentially mistaken about the system that we are all trying to be first in, especially if we have tried really hard?

Against all odds, the one rejected by the norms of religion and culture, Church and state, Jerusalem and Rome, the one crucified outside the walls, became the Lord of History! In truth, his life and death have turned human wisdom and judgment upside down. Paul later refers to it as "the folly of the cross" and often waxes eloquently on this theme (for example, 1 Corinthians 1:17-31). Gil Bailie calls it the virus of the gospel. It is enough to infect and save the world from itself and for the truth.

Once the victim becomes Lord, we will have a healthy mistrust of all attempts at domination, exclusion and victimization of others. If we were that wrong once about what is good and what is evil, we had best be suspicious about the claims of all righteous judgments. They might just be wrong again. Self-criticism is an outstanding characteristic of the Jewish tradition. They are one of the few peoples who incorporate into their sacred scriptures prophetic denunciations of *themselves*. This unusual capacity for critical thinking becomes a hallmark of Jesus' own relationship with his tradition, and one could say, it becomes a unique characteristic of groups influenced by the gospel. We call it the prophetic tradition. Without it, all groups and religions become idolatrous of themselves.

More positively, we are encouraged to welcome strangers, for by doing so, many people have entertained angels unaware (see Hebrews 13:2). As Jesus put it in his only description of the final judgment, "in so far as you did this to one of the least of these brothers of mine, you did it to me" (Matthew 25:40). One wonders what else will save us from our fear and accusation of one another, except one whose judgments are both upside-down and true—and whose mercy is everlasting. Fortunately, they are one and the same, a God who is both sanctuary and stumbling stone (see Isaiah 8:14).

We Need More and More of What Doesn't Work

It seems that only contact with the True Sacred will effectively inoculate us from the many forms of the false sacred. In the converse of the First Commandment we might say, if you do not worship the Lord as God, you will have strange gods before you. We might call the strange gods celebrities, jobs, self-image, security, money, family or power, but we honor and worship them with the same fervor that the saints reserved for God. It is amazing that folks do not see this.

Strange gods would be easy to recognize and dethrone if they were obviously evil, ugly stone statues, or the pagan gods of religions other than our own. But the substitutes for the True Sacred are probably as well denied and disguised today as they were in Jesus' time. The obvious idols are money, sex and power. The less obvious sacreds are even more devious precisely because they are usually partial reflections of the True Sacred. They give us just enough transcendence to sometimes inoculate us from the further journey toward their source. This is especially true in the lives of good, well-educated and well-intentioned people. One of the ironies of the gospel is that it is the well-bred people who fight Jesus the most. Let's look at some of our blockages:

Anything mysterious or unknown often feels spiritual, and people will speak in hushed tones of it as holy or sacred. Similarly, things which are secret, silent or hidden often have a numinous quality for many people. Consider how a good science fiction movie often inspires awe in its viewers.

That which is famous or well known or publicly observed has a larger-than-life quality for many people. In the absence of any real sacred stories, media events like public scandals, O.J. Simpson trials and rock stars take on a more-than-deserved quality. One could say that these have become the daily fuel of many peoples' entire lives. Cheap gas can keep a car going, but it eventually destroys the engine.

For some reason, that which is huge, large or powerful inspires awe and wonder in many people. We like the big. Stand at the bottom of a solid rock canyon, and you will somehow hear ancient voices and eternal meanings. Watch little boys' eyes when they see a strong man or young girls' eyes when they watch a beautifully dressed bride walk down the aisle. These are clearly images of gods and goddesses.

The natural, the wildness and freedom of nature changes many people into different kinds of people. All their lives they long to return, as if nothing else is real in comparison. Are they perhaps right? The Franciscan tradition always saw all creation as the footprints and fingerprints of God and therefore sacramental. This is true of many native spiritualities, and newly rediscovered creation spirituality too. It is much needed today if we are to rediscover the integrity of creation.

Anything which is old, ancestral or traditional ties one up with the timeless and the eternal. Listen to people's voices as they enter old ruins or uncover a piece of family history. They sigh.

The truly beautiful, the magnificent, the poetic all feel like ends in themselves—enough to satisfy. Joy and pleasure are surely promises and enticements, free samples that tell us we are on the track toward the same.

Surely God makes use of all these initial experiences of the holy. Yet philosophically there is no real ground for calling them sacred or holy. They are reflectors of light but not the source of light itself. This absolute and ultimate God-centeredness, this demand for the True Sacred, is at the heart of Jesus' teaching. His new world order rises and falls on this diamond edge, and it seems to be enough if only a few are convinced of it. Merely a "leaven" of true believers in the True Sacred is all that is needed to raise the whole loaf (see Matthew 13:33).

We Need a Yardstick

Unless we are confronted by true Otherness, we will spend our lives rattling around inside our own world of preferences without any criteria to evaluate or critique them. There is no north star to guide our little ship, lost in a sea of time. True transcendence, the Reign of God, becomes the measure by which all cultures and human actions are to be judged: "...you yourselves will sit on twelve thrones to judge the twelve tribes of Israel" (Matthew 19:28). This absence is the weakness and the continuing chaos of modern multiculturalism. Whose values prevail? By what criteria is this culture superior and that culture inferior? Are the measuring lines economic, political, aesthetic or familial? Although the world has suffered much from the various forms of Christian colonialism, the world has nothing to fear from either the message or the methods of the true Jesus. We are all winners in the Reign of God.

Jesus is teaching that *right relationship* is the ultimate and daily criterion. If a social order allows and encourages, and even mandates, good connectedness between people and creation, people and events, people and people, people and God, then you have a truly sacred culture: the Reign of God. The world as it would be if God were directly in charge would be a world of right relationship. It would not be a world without pain or mystery but simply a world where we would be in good contact with all things, where we would be connected and in communion. Conversely, the work of the Evil One is always to separate, divide and throw apart (*dia-bolical*).

It is all about union and communion, it seems, which means that it is also about forgiveness, letting go, service and lives of patience and simplicity. Who can doubt that this is the sum and substance of Jesus' teaching? He makes right relationship desirable, possible and the philosopher's stone by which everything else is to be weighed and judged.

In the Reign of God, the very motive for rivalry, greed and violence has been destroyed. Philosophically, we can see that the historical Jesus is the formal cause for the destruction of death. (A

11

formal cause gives shape and image and direction to a final effect.) Anthropologically, we can say that history and cultures have been slowly but definitely directed away from their justifications for violence and their rationalizations for greed by the life and teaching of Jesus. Psychologically, our death wishes are transmuted into a calming hope that feels like life-written-large. Scripturally, *"He went up to the heights, took captives"* (Ephesians 4:8). Spiritually, he unmasks our love affair with death by teaching us to recognize it as death and to weep over it. In those tears over the pain of Jesus and the pain of the world, we discover the lie, and in the same moment, the compassion that absorbs it. You cannot get much better than that.

Probably the imagery of Jesus as scapegoat is one of the more undeveloped themes in New Testament studies. Recent investigations of the Mishnah and other extra-biblical sources have helped us make a series of connections that were probably natural for first-century Judaism: The striking with the reed, the spitting on the scapegoat, the crowning, the entanglement with thorns, the scarlet cloak were all ways that the scapegoat was sent out into the desert. These rituals all developed from the original one mandated in Leviticus 16:7-10, 21-22. Perhaps we needed to see how universal and basic the scapegoating mechanism is for human culture before we could see the importance of Jesus' replacement of it. The passion accounts in the Gospels have little impact beyond that I should feel sad, unless we see Jesus as a cosmic archetype and answer. He is truly Job, Jeremiah, the sign of Jonah, the Suffering Servant of Isaiah, all in one. Jesus is everyman and everywoman. Jesus is the human dilemma—answered.

The Freedom That Sets Us Free

Crucial to Jesus' new world order are some very special understandings of freedom that must be clarified for the modern and postmodern mind. Without God's definition of freedom we will continue to use the gospel as if it were a product that can be bought, sold, imposed or attained. The gospel is not a competing ideology that is threatened by anything outside its pale. It is not one of the so-called, ten thousand things, but the gospel is that by which we see and evaluate the ten thousand things. It is the light of the world that illuminates the whole household (see Matthew 5:14); it is the yeast and not the whole loaf (see Matthew 13:33); it is the salt that gives flavor and nutrition to the much larger meal (see Matthew 5:13).

Once we can accept that Jesus has given us an illuminating lens by which to see and measure all things, we can no longer treat Christianity as a threat, nor allow it to be a threat, to human or cultural freedom. It is, in fact, true freedom's greatest ally, as will become clearer. The gospel is much more a process than a product, a style more than a structure, a person more than a production. It is a way of being in the world that will always feel like compassion, mercy and spaciousness—at least to honest and healthy people.

The gospel threatens nothing but death and *equally* critiques every culture. It is identical with no culture or institution, even the Church. As John's Gospel says so poetically, the Spirit blows where it will (see 3:8). How different and healing Western history could have been if we had received such gospel freedom and modeled it for others.

Jesus has not come to impose Christendom like an imperial system. One could say that the evidence for such later attempts is absolutely nil in the teaching of Jesus. In fact, he warns against it consistently. Wherever we have tried it, the long-term results have been disastrous—countries of baptized pagans or mere religious cultures that thought they were the Reign of God. The gospel flourishes in the realm of true freedom. I do not think that Jesus ever expected that the whole world would become formally Christian, but I do believe that his truth about right relationship, his proclamation of the power of powerlessness, is the message that will save the world from self-destruction and for an eternal truth. I do believe that Jesus is rightly called, therefore, the Savior of the World, and is able to do it through a minority position. Jesus always enters the imperial city on a donkey. He is the turning point of history, if this message is true.

Multiculturalism, which is the world's only possible future, has nothing to fear and a great deal to learn from the wisdom of the gospel. Unfortunately, it is going to take a few centuries to reconvince most of the world because of our past track record of

13

economic, political and spiritual colonialism. The gospel will always insist that means and ends must be in complete agreement, or the final end is always polluted. There is no way to peace. Peace is the way. There is no path toward love except by practicing love. War will always produce more war. Violence can never bring about true peace.

Much of the content of the Sermon on the Mount has to do with this agreement between means and ends. (It is one of the most ignored aspects of Jesus' teaching, and I am convinced it explains the attraction of many former Christians to Buddhism and nonviolent teaching. They had to leave home to find out what was hidden in their own closets.)

Furthermore, Jesus has a different understanding of personal freedom, too. Freedom is not the capacity to be what you are not, but the capacity to be fully who you already are, to develop your inherent self as much as God allows. The perfect and full freedom of a fig tree is to become a perfect and full fig tree. Thus Jesus curses one that does not (see Matthew 21:19). Contrary to our Western understanding since the French Revolution and the Enlightenment, it is not freedom for a fig tree to try to bear oranges or apples, or to try to be a horse or a wastebasket. Surely there is a certain freedom from constraint here, but this is not a very helpful kind of freedom. It only frustrates and finally destroys. It obstructs the fig tree's own fruitfulness and makes its own success impossible. It cannot work.

Many of us are like sick or dead fig trees, but with a happy face painted on our anemic apples shouting, "But I'm free!" Our addictive society has to do what it wants to do. The freedom offered by all great spiritual traditions is quite different: spiritual and true freedom is wanting to do what you have to do to become who you are. For some reason, humans rebel at what feels like an outer mandate. When they listen for awhile, they can often realize that it is also their deepest inner desire. *All things desire to be themselves* now has a different ring to it! No longer is it a scary search for private authenticity, but now a patient acceptance of truth. Such is the difference between wisdom and mere reaction, and it takes most of us awhile to get there.

We will not appreciate Jesus' loyalty to the Law and the

Prophets if we do not accept his deeper understanding of freedom. I'm afraid that the cry of the French Revolution, "Liberty, equality and fraternity," has formed us much more than the Jesus Revolution. His cry might instead be "Identity, justice and community." Think about the difference.

We also tend to think of freedom as freedom of movement and the liberty to choose between options. This is surely a good and important freedom. There is no indication that the great spiritual teachers, Jesus included, see it as essential, however. They seem to recognize that the world of preferences and possibilities does not of itself lead to wisdom, truth or even depth of experience. In fact, in the spiritual life the rule seems to be that less is more. There is almost no correlation between the amount of options and the amount of truth or goodness that one attains.

The saints usually seek to understimulate themselves, lessen their options, choose lives of poverty and flourish quite well in situations of imprisonment, persecution and opposition. Our notion of freedom as options and movement is a pleasant luxury, but not what Jesus is seeking when he goes into the desert, when he seems to limit himself in terms of family, marriage and a place to "lay his head," when he even accepts the limitations of a short ministry among uneducated people at a low period of religion in a country occupied by a foreign oppressor! That's not much freedom by *our* definition, but more than enough for him to say "the kingdom of God is among you" (Luke 17:21).

Apocalypse Now

It is commonly said that Jesus, and most of the New Testament authors, believed that the end of the world was right around the corner. Many passages in Paul and the Gospels would lead you to believe that this was their expectation. It *was*, but not in the way we think. It would be much closer to the truth to say that because the old order of the world (cultures built on money, power and mere religiosity) had now been so clearly exposed and defeated by the Jesus event, they thought it was only a matter of time until everybody would see through it all! I do suppose that both Jesus and Paul are still more than a little disappointed that it has taken so long to defeat the lie. I guess they were optimists about our capacity and desire for great truth.

It's all over can be understood in two very different ways: either it is all going to hell, or it is all becoming heaven. In either case, you stop taking the status quo as the final state of affairs. The burden of much modern thinking, which often leads to nihilism, is that it believes neither one. It gives the system too much credence on either the liberal or the conservative side. It has to fix and figure it all out by itself and by the latest research. No wonder it leads to nihilistic disbelief in anything. The daily evidence surely seems to be pointing to the first—it is all going to hell. The promise of God and the raising up of Jesus points, however, to the second: It is still becoming heaven, so do not give up and even do what you can to live the final reality now—and despite the evidence. We call it faith.

The apocalyptic readings that we come across in the Gospels (Matthew 24, Mark 13 and Luke 21:5-33) are not doomsday at all—unless your bottom line is wrong! They free you from propping up what is falling apart anyway; they keep you from wasting time on passing images; they keep you from putting your eggs into baskets with big holes in the bottom. They are not talking about the end of the world as much as the falling apart of worlds. Without such a clarifying and honest evaluation, we would live in a very incoherent world, an absurd and frightful world of constant loss and destruction of the very things that we thought were essential and even good. Now we know what to expect, what is worth rejoicing in and where to place our bets. Loss and death are part of the process.

Jesus' teaching is that this new world order has already begun, and he clearly seems to see himself as its herald, its inauguration and its personal assurance. No wonder he is forever central for us. He is the game plan in microcosmic form, but with one added difficulty: What is *now* in him is both now and *not yet* in us. Here is the source of almost all our problems with faith, trials and opposition. We must look at it closely.

Living in Between

All great religions advise a certain degree of necessary opposition, a refining of the question, a deep choosing of one's true position that comes only through time and trial. Some native religions say that human life must be lived on the edge of a knife. It must not be so comfortable that we lose contact with the struggle, and yet there must be enough security to sustain us through the trials. The promise of the Reign of God does not offer us pie in the sky, but just enough finger food to keep us nibbling and hoping for more: now. The promise of the Reign of God does not take away the opposition, but, in fact, assures it: not yet. That is the razor's edge of full faith existence. You must stay on the knife.

The old world order, however, is trying to create a society where we do not have to live on the edge of the knife. An economic culture is trying to eliminate as much inconvenience and discomfort as possible. It encourages increase in one tiny area, money, as the answer to all other areas. This most fragile premise takes much more faith to believe than the holistic truth of the gospel, yet most of the world seems to believe it. It promises to give you a relaxed and tension-free life, off that razor's edge. If it worked, I could see why people would buy it. But we need more and more of what does not work. This addiction is clearly the nature of economic cultures.

A political culture tries to eliminate all opposition and obstacle, as if life were attained by obliterating enemies and differences. Even the Church often descends to this pagan level, as Jesus calls it (see Matthew 20:25), when it resorts to dominative power and even punitive means to enforce its will. At that point, prayerful people know that there is little real trust in the presence of the Risen Jesus in history. He never relied upon enforcement in his lifetime; I do not know why he would change his strategy now. There is a soul knowledge, a victory of the Spirit, that comes only from engagement, patience, prayer, insight and inner transformation. It is never attained by mere political victories or control of outcomes. In fact, when a Christian needs to ensure outcomes, you know they are outside the realm of faith. When we do not need to control the future, we are in a very creative and liminal space where God is most free to act in our lives. Faith seems to be the attitude that Jesus

17

most praises in people, maybe because it makes hope and love possible.

There is no such thing as a victory of the Spirit if it is attained by coercion, mere mandate or social pressure. Paul said it in great urgency and anger to his community at Galatia: Are you foolish enough to resort to the law for what you began in the Spirit? Has grace been wasted on you? If this is so, it most certainly has been wasted (see 3:3). Wow! How did that become lost in the Tradition? A political culture, like the former Soviet Union, will always use power in totalitarian ways to achieve its purposes. We can never expect Caesar to do Christ's work. We can never proclaim the exodus from Pharaoh's palace. If we try, as surely we have, it will always be on his terms. You would think we would know that by now.

A religious culture is one that is trapped in such a confusion. It mixes up belief in God with cultural order and institutional stability. It needs and wants a great policeman in the sky to keep everything in line. I can surely understand the need, especially when it works rather efficiently and does keep people at some early stages of needed morality. A religious culture has much to recommend it, sort of like John the Baptist in his early stages. He baptized in water, enforced some needed moralities, and, according to Jesus, neither ate nor drank (see Matthew 11:18). He was a good and religious man, as far as that goes, yet Jesus makes a most amazing statement that we have usually glossed over: "[Of] all the children born to women, there has never been anyone greater than John the Baptist; yet the least in the kingdom of Heaven is greater than he" (Matthew 11:11)

One wonders if a religious culture, symbolized very well by John the Baptist, is not the most common precursor for the full Kingdom of God, symbolized by Jesus. I personally believe that is the usual pattern. Religion is the best, and it is the worst (for the corruption or misuse of the best is the worst). We need religious cultures that are not afraid to speak of God, but we do not need religious cultures that use and misquote God for their own purposes, or become ends in themselves. Like John the Baptist, they must be ready to become smaller so Christ can become larger (see John 3:30). Such cases of institutional or national forgetfulness are rather rare, I am afraid. Some would insist that the very nature of institutions is to perpetuate and protect themselves, even Church institutions.

The Reign of God never sells humanity short. In Paul's later description, he forbids that we trivialize God's plan: "A privilege of yours must not be allowed to give rise to harmful talk; for it is not eating and drinking that make the kingdom of God, but the saving justice, the peace and joy brought by the Holy Spirit" (Romans 14:16-17). There is a certain challenge that is proper to, and needed by, human nature. We seem to need some obstacles that are worthy of our energy and passion. The soul is not slovenly and flourishes only in the presence of a certain opposition. As Simone Weil put it, truth and affliction are necessary allies. When Jesus offers the great repayment for loss of house, brothers, sisters, father, children and land (see Mark 10:30), he adds only one extra reward to the promise of a hundredfold return—and that is— persecution! That doesn't sound like a reward—unless communion and love are the final goals.

There Is Only the Supernatural

Near the end of the Old Testament, the Prophet Zechariah says that when God's day comes, there will be no distinction between sacred and profane, temple and marketplace: Even the horse bells will be inscribed with the word "sacred," and in the Temple of Yahweh the very cooking pots will be as fine as the sprinkling bowls at the altar (see 14:20). The Reign of God is not about churchiness at all. It has everything to do with everything. In fact, as we listen to Jesus' images and examples, it appears that it is the world of house and field and job and marriage where we are converted to right relationship. The secular has become the place where we encounter the True Sacred. As Catholic theology would say, it is a sacramental universe. It is the domestic Church that converts us; it is the job of the liturgical Church to send us back there. It is the unexciting world of details, diapers and "women who have lost one dime" (see Luke 15:8-10) that appears to offer the teachable moment for Jesus. It is much more, it seems, than the world of stipends, sermons and sacristies, which tend to become

19

their own industry.

An Upside-Down World

There is a telling phrase that is used in the Acts of the Apostles to describe this new sect that is upsetting the old world order in Thessalonika. The Christians of that town were dragged before the city council and called "[t]he people who have been turning the whole world upside down...[t]hey have broken Caesar's edicts" (Acts 17:6-7). You are not called before the city council for mere inner beliefs or new attitudes unless they are also upsetting the social order. We will see that the import of Jesus' teaching and almost all of his healing and nature miracles were a rearranging of social relationships and therefore of social order. You do not go around eating with the underclass, touching the untouchables, sending lepers back into polite society as a testimony against them (see Mark 1:44), and collaborating with upstarts down at the river without turning traditional societies upside down. City councils are not places that we go for profound wisdom; their job is to hold societies together where they are always held together—at the level of conventional wisdom—the way we always do it here in Thessalonika. One of the major weaknesses of the Christian understanding of Jesus is that we really do not understand what it was that made Jesus worth killing. It was not because he walked around saying "I am God."

There are four principal areas of conventional wisdom that Jesus seems to either ignore, oppose or even subvert: family, possessions, status and the very nature of sacrificial religion. We will see that these were enough to get him killed. We will be looking for this alternative wisdom of Jesus in the rest of this book.

Note

[1] I want to acknowledge my gratitude to the important anthropological work of Gil Bailie (*Violence Unveiled*, Crossroad, 1995), and his own mentor, René Girard (*Violence and the Sacred*, Johns Hopkins University Press, 1979; *Things Hidden Since the Foundation of the World*, Stanford University Press, 1987). They have confirmed for me what Karl Rahner always insisted, that for those of us from the

Judeo-Christian Tradition, theology and anthropology are the same thing. God is revealing who God is through human history and culture; the only God we know is the God we have met in our history.

CHAPTER TWO

Not Business As Usual

He was still speaking to the crowds when suddenly his
mother and his brothers were standing outside and were
anxious to have a word with him. But to the man who told
him this Jesus replied, "Who is my mother? Who are my
brothers?" And stretching out his hand towards his
disciples he said, "Here are my mother and my brothers.
Anyone who does the will of my Father in heaven is my
brother and sister and mother." (Matthew 12:46-50)

To challenge family was really shocking to a culture based on
the kinship system. In fact, a pivotal point in Matthew's
Gospel, the symbolic middle of the Gospel, is the scene where
Jesus creates a new definition of family.

Jesus switches sides. He's on the inside of a house teaching his
disciples when his mother shows up. Mary is standing *outside* with
"his brothers" and the word is sent to Jesus *inside* that his mother
and brothers want to see him. And he says, " 'Who is my mother?
Who are my brothers?' And stretching out his hand towards his
disciples he said, 'Here are my mother and my brothers. Anyone
who does the will of my Father in heaven is my brother and sister
and mother' " (Matthew 12:47b-50; see also Mark 3:31-35).

Jesus has in a moment turned upside down the whole bloodline
family system, even at the risk of slighting his mother! That's
utterly shocking and unacceptable to his culture. Jesus says it's not
blood that makes family; it's trust, union and commitment. He has
redefined family in a kinship-based culture (which is often the
shape of religious cultures). From that point, after Matthew 12,
everything turns to those outside—who are, of course, invited
"inside" (where Mary and Jesus' "brothers" surely are).

The scene is presented as a scandalous passage so you can't

miss the point: How could he dare to consider his own mother an outsider? Well, he is willing for you to think that so you will redefine what family is. Jesus opposes conventional wisdom so much that he has redefined the family in terms of the universal family of love. Looking back two thousand years later, how many wars have been justified by kinship? Jesus broke that addiction to false patriotism, loyalty and nationality.

Jesus also questioned conventional wisdom in regard to wealth and possessions. That should be obvious, but it hasn't been at all. The Church itself, which was supposed to be a new social ethic, became very comfortable with wealth and possessions after Constantine made it the state religion in A.D. 313. We moved from underground catacombs to princely basilicas.

I realize what Dominic and Francis were trying to do in the thirteenth century by creating a new kind of clergy who would take a vow of poverty and not be a part of the ruling class or wealth system. The initials we put after our names as Franciscans are *O.F.M.*, which stand for *Order of Friars Minor*. In modern language, it would be "brothers of the lower class." Mendicants— beggars—are, by definition, outside the production/consumption economy.

Francis switched sides from the upper class to the lower class, because he knew that only from the side of powerlessness could one be entrusted with the gospel. Those who stay on the side of power have consistently misused and misinterpreted the gospel. Francis was a sociological genius without knowing it, especially in understanding how the gospel could be heard, how the gospel had to be preached and understood. In subsequent centuries every religious order saw that. They all took the vow of poverty as an *essential* part of the gospel life. The vow clearly was a choice by a community and by an individual to opt out of the economic system. Unfortunately, we eventually became corporately wealthy and now we have our portfolios. Isn't that a shame? How it turns around: Take the vow of poverty to opt out of the system, and then be sucked back into it!

The third area in which Jesus assaults conventional wisdom is in the area of social and religious recognition, the whole honor/shame system. He refuses to abide by it. He refuses to live up to what is considered honorable and refuses to shame what people consider shameful. (If that is not apparent in your reading of the Gospels, read them again.) This does not gain him many friends. It's perhaps the thing that most bothers the priests and the elders. In response to his ignoring the debt codes and purity codes, they decided to kill him (see Mark 3:6, 11:18; Matthew 12:14; Luke 19:47; John 11:53). Even his family thought he was crazy (see Mark 3:21)!

Every culture and Church has such honor/shame systems—even libertines who think they don't.

The New World Order

Chapter One discussed a new religious culture. But Jesus' vision has political implications, too. When Jesus talked about the Kingdom of God, he was talking about an utterly different way of relating with one another than human society as we know it.

For example, the decades following World War II established a world order with which most of us have lived most of our adult lives. It was the Cold War alignment, conveniently blessed by our theological understandings: We in the West were the good guys and the Communists were the bad guys.

We chose this understanding because the ego always wants to feel superior. The high moral ground the West took in the Cold War—along with our nuclear weapons—gave us a false sense of security. That all ended in 1991 with the collapse of the Soviet Union. Now our Western leaders are scrambling to define a "new world order," in the words of former President George Bush. And I suspect that we will look again to terms of power to define ourselves. I doubt very much that George Bush, Bill Clinton or any other major political leader would align a new world order in terms of cooperation, trust, service and redemptive suffering!

My point is this: For all the talk of a new world order, it's simply the old world order. The politicians had no right to steal that phrase, especially when there is nothing *new* about it! The new world order—the Reign of God—is the heart of the New Testament, and it's a phrase to be taken seriously. Yet we have failed to understand the coming of Jesus as the dawn of a new age.

For most Christians, life in the new age has been business as usual.

What is the new age Jesus talks about? In Matthew 19:23-26, Jesus describes the danger of riches. Peter then speaks up. "What about us?" he asks. "We have left everything and followed you. What are we to have, then?" (see Matthew 19:27). It's an anxious question, because Jesus has just told them that anyone who leaves everything is going to do OK. "Jesus said to them, 'In truth I tell you, *when everything is made new again...*' " (Matthew 19:28a, emphasis added). He just assumes that things can be and will be constructed differently. Such a vision seems to be his starting point—even more than his practical goal. One has to share the "dream of God" before we know how to live and where to look for the truth.

"When all is made new" in the original Greek phrase of the New Testament authors includes the word *palingenesia*—a unique word. It's rendered literally as "regeneration, a new genesis, an utterly new beginning," or, perhaps best, "a totally new birth in a totally new world." It's the only time the word is used in the Gospels.

The Acts of the Apostles will use another Greek phrase, *apocatastasis*, translated in the Jerusalem Bible as "universal restoration." That's in Peter's first sermon, and he's grown up a bit since Matthew's Gospel. Now he courageously preaches that God "will send you the Christ he has predestined, that is Jesus, whom heaven must keep till the universal restoration comes which God proclaimed, speaking through his holy prophets" (Acts 3:21). In later theological language this term was used to describe the restoration of all creation at the end, the reconciliation of all things in Christ (see Colossians 1:20). What a hopeful and positive apocalypse that would be! I personally love to believe that is the real meaning of the victory of Christ and the final resurrection.

What we will discover in the New Testament text, especially in Matthew's Gospel, is this new world order, a new age, a promised hope. This new age was not something the early Christians first understood as happening at the end of history; rather, it was ushered in by the teaching of Jesus. *Jesus was undercutting the system of human society, refusing to take it seriously—while continuing to love and serve it.*

Scripture scholar John P. Meier, speaking of the Sermon on the

26

Mount, writes in *A Marginal Jew: Rethinking the Historical Jesus* (New York: Doubleday, 1991) that Jesus "was not proclaiming the reform of the world; he was proclaiming the end of the world." And that's the point of this book, right here in our opening pages: Jesus is not presenting a new program for human society. Jesus refuses to accept society on its own terms; he refuses to offer it allegiance as it is. When we read all of the apocalyptic announcements of Jesus, how everything is going to fall apart, how the sun will fall from the heavens, we're reading that the world *as we know it* must and will end. We speak here not so much of a final end of history but an end to our own personally constructed worlds.

That's an experience that must first happen spiritually. It must happen in our psyche, in our relationships and in our culture. One day it just happens. It's the moment of conversion, when all of a sudden you realize—not just in your head but also in your guts—that everything in this world is passing away. All is impermanent, socially constructed and, in that sense, illusory.

The sad thing for many of us is that it doesn't happen until we confront death, usually the death of a loved one. In my own life I recently became aware of the mortality of two friends with cancer, and as I heard their sad news I fell behind a haze: "It's all passing away. Nothing lasts," I thought. When you're young, it's very hard to believe that; it dawns on you the older you get and the more you experience death, failure and what the New Testament calls the cross.

But Jesus is not talking just about the death of friends. He means that the whole gospel can't really be heard until you recognize the final, utter truth of this world. It's not a morbid recognition, but it is nonetheless an acceptance that everything except God is relative and is passing away. Any economic system that your government offers you is OK, but don't put too much trust in it: It's not any final answer. You can eat all the tofu you want and you will still die. All the guns in America will not give you the security of God.

Whether you vote for Democrats, Republicans or Independents, don't really think any of them can usher in the Kingdom of God (even when the newly elected Bill Clinton spoke of a "New Covenant!"). And if you think, "Who could be that naive?" don't forget that Americans have come very close to that kind of naiveté for most of their history.

Americans, like few other peoples, have known two hundred years of massive cultural idolatry. We think that our country, our form of government, our way of doing things fell straight from heaven, as if it were God's plan for the world. If everyone would live like Americans the world would be happy, we think. Maybe people don't say it that way, but believe me, I know as a preacher the shock on people's faces when I dare to question it! That tells me they believe it. It is a cultural myth, which means it is unquestioned: It's a way of thinking, written between the lines and in the margins.

Idols, like cultural myths, are always disguised, if not totally invisible to the worshiper. If we could see their falsity, we would, of course, know that they are not God. So false gods, idols, must always dress up as a cultural virtue like success, love of country or hard work. These loyalties, either hidden or expressed, must be exposed for the gods that they are. Until this happens, there will be nothing really *new* and God's dream cannot show itself.

Finally, what is most amazing and therefore most overlooked by most Christians, is how much of Jesus' teaching is concerned with subverting conventional understandings of religion. It is, in fact, such a total critique of almost all early-stage religion that it would be easy to view Jesus as antireligious. His anti-Temple shenanigans are, in fact, where he seems to cross the line. Much of the preceding Gospel text has him intentionally heading toward Jerusalem where he has no doubt "the elders and the chief priests and the scribes" (Mark 8:31) will kill him. His good-boy disciples refuse to believe it, and either miss the point, change the subject or actively oppose him every time he brings it up. (See Mark 8:31—10:45.) Only an unnamed woman, clearly outside the circles of religious power, sees the handwriting on the wall. She knows what he is doing and where it will lead: "She has done what she could: she has anointed my body beforehand for its burial" (Mark 14:8).

His religious culture is finally what gets him killed, for he is living in a religious culture. The bottom line here is God-talk that legitimizes an in-group and increasingly marginalizes more and more unacceptable people. The outcasts have to leave the Temple and go out to the river Jordan for the forgiveness of sin. For Jesus to join in John's baptism at that location outside of town was a symbolic critique of the whole Temple system and its lend-lease brokerage system. For a religion that had clear controls on how sin could be forgiven, we have John pouring it out like free river water. No wonder the scribes and Pharisees came out to observe and threaten (see John 1:24-25). Their monopoly on God was being ignored by an announcement of living and ever-available water, from the very river that symbolized deliverance and freedom (see Joshua 3:10-17).

Subverting the Old World Order

Jesus' new world order is utterly subverting the old world order. This is what makes people so furious: Jesus simply ignores the systems of values and righteousness that are so important to them. That is much more subversive than it might seem on the surface. For example, by Jesus' reckoning, why would anyone try to become rich? It doesn't make a bit of sense once you know the really real. It is much more effective than mere fire and brimstone sermons on the evil of riches.

That experience of the really Real—the "Kingdom" experience—is the heart of Jesus' teaching. It's Reality with a capital *R*, the very bottom line, the pattern-that-connects. It's the goal of all true religion, the experience of the Absolute, the Eternal, what *is*. The Kingdom is Jesus' way of describing God's dream for the world.

Jesus talked about this dream constantly. In Matthew 9:17, Jesus says, "Nor do people put new wine into old wineskins; otherwise, the skins burst, the wine runs out, and the skins are lost. No; they put new wine into fresh skins and both are preserved." That's a very commonsense image for Jesus' agrarian peasant audience. Such colorful, real images—symbolic talk—communicate instantly.

Jesus' image is this: "I'm going to give you a new vision of the world that you will taste like new wine, but it isn't going to make a bit of difference unless you have some new wineskins. If there are not new structures that reflect the new attitude, then even the attitude will be lost. *Both* container and contents must be renewed—or they will both be lost."

We have traditionally tried to preach a gospel largely of words, attitudes and inner salvation experiences. People say they are saved, they're "born again," yet how do we really know if someone is saved? Do they love the poor? Are they free from their egos? Are they patient in the face of persecution? Those might be real indicators.

A so-called new attitude inside an old world order that we accept uncritically will finally dilute and even destroy the very attitude. It's not enough to talk about some kind of new inebriating wine, some new wisdom, without new wineskins, new structures, a new world order. As Dorothy Day often said in her perfect Kingdom style, "Nothing is going to change until we stop accepting this dirty, rotten system!" That's not to say that people are not of goodwill, or that they are not journeying, that God is not going to save them. God will save them. But we need to be honest about the impact—or lack of impact—of the gospel on Western civilization, on the world. That which has become standard and normative must first be called into serious question.

I preach occasionally in Europe, in the so-called Christian nations who gave us what we thought was the gospel. It's not a very pretty picture; if you've been there you know what I mean. Largely empty cathedrals are filled with golden angels and rococo statues. We have there the outer structure, but there's no community inside the structure. More and more of the churches are empty, especially of men and the young.

One can make a strong case for the Christian nations being the most militaristic ones on earth—the most greedy, the most untrue to the teacher they claim to follow. That's not to say our ancestors didn't have faith, that Grandma and Grandpa were not good people. But by and large we did not produce a Christian *culture*. We produced some wonderfully liberated saints and Christian individuals. They tried to create some new wineskins, but often the Church itself resisted their calls to any structural reform. Take even the father of my religious community, Saint Francis—he wasn't even dead yet when we moved him out of leadership and exiled him because we were afraid to take him seriously!

Assisi is another good example. Both the Rule and the

Testament of Saint Francis tell us: Don't ever own or build your own buildings. Seek little churches at best, where you can stay "as pilgrims and strangers." But have you ever been to Assisi? Poor Francis and Clare were so hated by the establishment of their time that they moved outside the walls of Assisi. Now there's a giant church on one end of town where Francis is buried and on the other end of town a giant church where Clare is buried! Talk about divine irony! The town has been living off them for eight hundred years. They're selling little Francis and Clare dolls, but do they really do what Francis and Clare did? Probably not.

That's not to single Assisi out; we're all the same. It's easier to talk about the wine without the wineskins, to talk about salvation theories without any new world order. In honesty, the European nations that call themselves Christian base their society, as we all do, entirely upon structures of domination and control: racism, sexism, class, power and money. They're built on all the things Jesus told us not to build on. That's a little bit of new wine in some very old wineskins.

It might be a little cynical, but you could almost figure out what Jesus said by looking at our history and naming the opposite of what we did! We keep worshiping the messenger, keeping Jesus up on statues and images, so we can avoid what Jesus said. It's the best smokescreen in the world! We just keep saying, "We love Jesus." The more we talk about Jesus, the less we'll do what he said. That's the way the ego fools itself. And in this case, it's the way culture, nations and even the churches have fooled themselves.

The Symbolism of the Temple and the End of Worlds

Jesus' sayings about the end of the world are a key to understanding his radical message. But before looking at these passages, it's important to talk about images and sacred mythology. Part of the reason why we've become so confused by the Scriptures is we no longer understand sacred mythology. Popular understanding of this took a big jump with the PBS interviews of Bill Moyers with Joseph Campbell. Campbell, who fought Catholicism all his life, also admitted that it gave him his fascination with images. He bitterly regretted the liturgical changes of Vatican II. And, although his vision of Catholicism was severely limited, he had a point: We used to draw upon an immense treasure house of right-brain, nonrational, translucent images. We used incense a lot more then, for example, with its intense aroma and mystifying visual presence. We had music—Gregorian chant—that hauntingly emphasized the otherworldly aspects of life. We've lost that to some degree during the past thirty years. Though we wouldn't want to turn things back, our loss of right-brain liturgical action is a great loss to an entire generation of youth and overzealous reformers.

Yet images are very powerful and essential to religion. As Carl Jung, the ground-breaking Swiss psychiatrist, said, transformation only takes place in the presence of images, not concepts. Until we *reimagine* our God, ourselves, our world, nothing ever happens. People born before the scientific rational revolution of the last few hundred years knew how to read sacred literature. They knew that time-tested mythology is always true and that the truth is conveyed in the symbols and stories themselves.

We moderns, tainted by the scientific method, have forgotten how to read sacred literature. We look for empirical truth when the stories are full of mythical, symbolic images. In order to understand our Scriptures, we must be willing to look for the symbols, *to treat sacred stories as powerful, truth-bearing stories, not historical reporting.*

With that in mind, let us take up Jesus' Apocalyptic Discourse in Matthew 24. It starts with "Jesus left the Temple." Though we tend to jump over that first verse to get to the center of the text, we need to stop there. The Temple, after all, represents the entire system wrapped up in one great big structure. Here's the entire first verse: "Jesus left the Temple, and as he was going away his disciples came up to draw his attention to the Temple buildings." The disciples are always doing things like that! It's the end of the Gospel, the twenty-fourth out of twenty-eight chapters, and they still haven't gotten the point! He's leaving the Temple and they're admiring its architecture.

The juxtaposition of phrases shouts at anyone who reads sacred literature well. The disciples are still rooted in the entire system the Temple represents. They're still marveling at the Temple structure.

And Jesus' reply is, "You see all these [stones]? In truth I tell you, not a single stone here will be left on another" (Matthew 24:2b). It's all going to fall apart. Will you stop putting your trust in it?

The next verse gives us a hint: "And while he was sitting on the Mount of Olives the disciples came and asked him when they were by themselves, 'Tell us, when is this going to happen, and what sign will there be of your coming and of the end of the world?' " (24:3). Again there is a clever juxtaposition of phrases: when *Christ's presence* (*parousia*) is experienced, it *is* the end of the world as we have known it!

We normally read Matthew 24 on the last four Sundays of the Church year to scare us and remind us that the world's going to end. But Matthew's message is communicated on both levels simultaneously: He's talking about the end of the world, but Matthew is also talking about the end of worlds. How appropriate that the last Sundays of the Church year name the end of worlds before the new world comes in Advent and Christmas!

If you've ever gotten to a point in your life when you let go of a world, you understand this text. We cannot welcome the presence, the parousia, the full coming of Christ until we've let go of the old. We've lived under the illusion that we could have both: We could idolatrously worship this world order and at the same time say, "Thy Kingdom come." Yet we can't say, "Thy Kingdom come" unless we're willing to say, "My kingdom go." Remember this the next time you hear the apocalyptic readings of November. Don't be afraid to let the heavens be shaken (see Matthew 24:29) and to abandon the defense of your personal temple and cultural Jerusalem.

Shaking the Foundation: The Letting Go of Worlds

Unless you're willing to let go of your self-created ego worlds, you will not see the Kingdom in your midst. The ego, by nature, is conservative. It strives to conserve, to maintain itself. That translates into seeking a comfort zone to live within and staying there. Once we find that place where we feel secure, we may do anything to maintain it!

I remember an episode from the TV show *60 Minutes*. An

investigative team was checking out people in America who make bogus repairs. The investigators put secret markings inside of appliances, on parts that might be replaced during a repair. When they picked up the appliances from some repair shops, they could tell by taking off the appliance cover that the original parts were still in the appliance, even though the expensive repair bills listed replacement parts.

The investigators came back to the shops, cameras rolling, to present their evidence. "No, I didn't do that!" the repairmen claimed. "Here is proof!" the TV crew countered. "No, I didn't do that," the repairmen lied again. I sat there watching this in disbelief! Every single one of the repairmen denied the evidence before his eyes! It shows how capable we are of immense denial when the ego is involved.

Sadly, perhaps a more common example of this happens in homes where abuse is taking place. Often alcoholism is there, too. Many women who finally come to crisis shelters, badly bruised, are in massive denial about their own abusers. They refuse to believe what is happening to them until they are so injured that they require medical help. Even then, many will continue to deny a pattern of abuse—"He just got carried away," they may say.

The Twelve-Step programs have shown us how widespread this denial can be in our lives. We can become so self-protective we will lie through our teeth, as the saying goes. For the person—or the Church or the society—caught in the trap of denial, security becomes an idol. We become incapable of loving and incapable of truth.

That world of denial and false security is the old world order Jesus is undercutting. Jesus talks about this undercutting in terms of salt and leaven. The gospel is like a virus set loose in the world. There's no way to get toothpaste back into the tube; there's no way to get the horse back in the barn; there's no way to undo Kingdom people. I see it wherever I go: people who know what's real, who have experienced the eternal and absolute. They know it's all relative and impermanent and refuse to worship any system. They are trapped—and it often feels like a trap!—in the truth.

In Matthew 24, Jesus says, "Take care that no one deceives you, because many will come using my name and saying, 'I am the

Christ,' and they will deceive many. You will hear of wars and rumours of wars; see that you are not alarmed, for this is something that must happen, but the end will not be yet. For nation will fight against nation, and kingdom against kingdom. There will be famines and earthquakes in various places. All this is only the beginning of the *birthpangs*" (24:4-8, emphasis added).

Jesus is presenting an image of something that is painful but is bringing about something better. The price of bringing something better is to go through the pain of birth. Do you think if we'd had a more feminine image of God that we would have understood creation as labor and giving birth? Much of patriarchal Christian interpretation has been trying to avoid pain, trying to avoid being poor, trying to avoid powerlessness. That's why we couldn't hear Jesus. If we had had an image of God as the great mother who is giving birth—as in Romans 8:22—I think history as process, pain, patience, guided destiny would have come more naturally. As it is, we have seen history as a linear obstacle course, something to be conquered, exploited and won.

A woman who has borne a child understands something I will never understand. I will never understand the innate connection between pain and life. When I give talks on male spirituality, I encourage men to consider this: Why were most tribal initiation rites for men? Why weren't they for women? Why did most peoples discover that men have to be *taught* about failure and suffering? Why did the vast majority of peoples create rites of passage, scarification, ordeals, vision quests and circumcision for young men? It seems that men, in particular, must be taught that life is hard, that humans are not in control, that death is a reality.

Why not the woman? Because a woman knows in her body when bleeding happens that there's something dying and yet something stirring. Some girls surprised at the onset of menstruation remember thinking they *were* dying! In her cycles and in childbirth, a woman can learn more about life than some men ever do. Women are able to make an early body connection that a man never makes. Along with their subservient position in most societies, women have a symbolic head start in understanding the Paschal Mystery of death and resurrection.

At the beginning of the Apocalyptic Discourse quoted

previously, there was mention of famine and earthquakes. Of course, every time there is an earthquake, someone is trying to figure if this is the "biggie." One could cook up evidence every three years that now is the time for the apocalypse. We'll see at the end of Matthew 24 that we shouldn't waste our time trying to figure that out: That isn't the point. The end is all the time, and it never stops. This quaking of the earth is repeated by Matthew both at the death of Jesus (27:51), the centurion's act of faith (27:54) and the resurrection (28:2). In each case, it is now a new world and these acts are at the epicenter.

In the Discourse, a few verses further along: "Immediately after the distress of those days the sun will be darkened, the moon will not give its light, the stars will fall from the sky and the powers of the heavens will be shaken. And then the sign of the Son of man will appear in heaven; then, too, all the peoples of the earth will beat their breasts; and they will see the Son of man coming on the clouds of heaven with power and great glory" (Matthew 24:29-30).

It's almost like a mythological description of depression. Have you ever had a day when it all doesn't make any sense? Emptiness has to precede fullness. Usually our old securities have to be wrested from us before we will move into the new. We seldom do it deliberately. Spirituality is always about letting go—not just in Christianity, but in Judaism, Islam, Hinduism, Buddhism. All the great world religions at their higher levels teach the mystery and the art of letting go. You let go, and hopefully collapse back into your true self, into who you really are. The work of religion is to guide us on the path of the fall and onto the path of the return. What Jesus is painting here with his words is a cosmic liturgy, a cosmic image of everything falling apart. Out of that emptiness comes the possibility of a new kind of fullness.

"Take the fig tree as a parable," he says; "as soon as its twigs grow supple and its leaves come out, you know that summer is near. So with you when you see all these things: know that [the Son of Man] is near, right at the gates. In truth I tell you, before this generation has passed away, all these things will have taken place" (Matthew 24:32-35).

It's interesting to note Jesus' style here. He doesn't quote Scripture; that's why his authority is not like the authority of the scribes and the Pharisees (see Matthew 7:29). He doesn't quote "papal encyclicals." He most often uses *nature* as an authority. He points to clouds, sunsets, sparrows, lilies, corn in the field, leaves unfolding, several kinds of seeds, oxen in a ditch!

Nature instructs us everywhere. Look and learn how to see. Look and see the rhythm, the seasons, the life and death of things. That's your teaching, that's creation's plan in front of you. The new world is constantly coming into being as the old world passes. *Nothing* lives in nature unless something else dies, and it often happens slowly and is unseen—unless you learn how to see.

Christians have tried to figure out why the world didn't end the way Jesus seemed to be saying it would. Remember, though, the Gospels were written after the Temple was already destroyed. Jesus uses Temple imagery, but the reason it's going to happen before this generation passes away is because it happens in every generation.

Jesus is incorrect chronologically/historically, but he is absolutely correct in terms of the soul. "Sky and earth will pass away, but my words will never pass away" (Matthew 24:35). All you can do, Jesus goes on to say, is *be ready*! In fact, the next forty-four verses leading up to the judgment scene are all metaphors of readiness, awakening, vigilance and cunning (Noah, peasants, property owners, stewards, bridesmaids and entrepreneurs).

It is most unfortunate that, like naughty children, we have read these apocalyptic passages almost exclusively in terms of warning, threat and dire prediction. That's a sad example of what happens when we read the sacred story mechanically instead of soulfully. Most of this chapter in Matthew is a call to be alert and awake, but we have heard it as Jesus telling us to be afraid—the exact thing he spoke against.

Spirituality is about being ready. All the spiritual disciplines of your life—prayer, study, meditation or ritual, religious vows—are there so you can break through to the eternal. Spirituality is about awakening the eyes, the ears, the heart so you can see what's always happening right in front of you.

One of the men's retreats I lead is on the hero's journey. I ask the men, How do you prepare for being a hero? Do you go to hero school? Do you decide to do risky or dramatic things? No, that will just get you into the ego. All you can do is be ready, and God will create your heroism—which won't even feel heroic to you.

I tell people in discernment on retreats: Just ask the Lord to ready your heart. Don't try to build your own door or heroically create your own project. Don't even go search for the door you're supposed to go through. Just ask that when the door shows itself, you'll have the eyes to recognize it and the courage to walk through it. Other times I tell them, "Don't push the river. Just remain in the flow." After reading this book and getting all fired up about Jesus' radical message, don't set out to open some big soup kitchen! (Unless you put down this book and the first thing someone tells you is, "we need a soup kitchen"—maybe *that* would be a beckoning!) Often we do God's work for our own ego purposes. In reality we probably all start there, and the wondrous truth is that God even uses such things to good purpose.

"So stay awake," Jesus says, "because you do not know the day when your master is coming. You may be quite sure of this, that if the householder had known at what time of the night the burglar would come, he would have stayed awake and would not have allowed anyone to break through the wall of his house" (Matthew 24:42-43).

What a wonderful symbol of God as a burglar, the divine thief! Our patterns and character present a formidable armor against the gospel. The only way the truth gets into any of our lives is by God's trickery, when our guard is down. (That's why you've got to listen to your dreams: because our character armor is down when we are sleeping.) Our operative God-image would probably be far more attractive and lively if we had accepted such prankish or trickster relationships with God. The God of Jesus is clearly much more than a stern moralist or divine policeman. Daringly, Jesus puts God "outside the law" as one who comes into our lives by stealth and cunning, the burglar who comes in the night and steals our soul in spite of ourselves!

God will always get at you on the run. The ego is moving straight ahead into success and power, into good name, achievement and all the other stupid things that we race after. Then once in a while you glimpse out of the corner of your eye what really matters. Gotcha!

A Zen master frequently claps his hands to break the trance, the collective illusion that we are all a part of. Perhaps the old bell at the Consecration of the Mass was attempting to do the same. Let go of the private dream for the dream of God.

Most of us live in the past, carrying our hurts, guilts and fears. We have to face the pain we carry, lest we spend the rest of our lives running away from it or letting it run us. But the only place you'll ever meet the real is now-here. It's the hardest place for us to live, the place where we're most afraid to live, because it feels so empty and boring. Now-here almost always feels like nowhere, and that's precisely where we must go.

Silence is what allows the old world order to become unnecessary, and you really don't know that until you are silent. I recently had the luxury of a forty-seven-day contemplative retreat, where I escaped from this world order. I didn't need to depend upon it, believe it or listen to it. I didn't play its games or carry out its roles. That is the historic meaning in so many mythologies of the hermit.

Jesus becomes a hermit when he goes off to the desert. John the Baptist lives in the desert. The desert is where you go apart from the world order as it is. It's where you simply stop being trapped in the world's addictive patterns. If you are addicted to the world's or your own patterns, you really need to go apart; otherwise you'll never stop sleepwalking.

It makes me wonder how many people today are going to get out of the trap. With earphones playing music all day and billboards in front of us all the time, will we ever know what the real is? I'm not talking here about who's going to heaven and who's not going to heaven. That language seems to cause more harm than good. In fact, it would be better to get rid of that language for good: It really doesn't help you understand what Jesus was up to. We've got to know that what Jesus is talking about, first and foremost, is how do you enter into the real *now*. Jesus gives us real eyes to realize where the Real lies. (Say that last sentence aloud—that might help you remember!)

The Mustard Seed/Weed Parable of the Kingdom

It's very hard for us to understand our world without a philosophy of progress. Yet I think Jesus lives in such a world. Jesus realizes that what he's talking about is going to come rather modestly. That's hard for us to hear because we've been raised in a world of progress and goals. Men and women all have been loaded with expectations to grow up and become certain things, whether domestic or professional. We are what we do, we think. Fortunately our inherent Christ nature is not a goal to be achieved, but an inheritance.

Jesus doesn't think like a typical American. His parables from Matthew 13 in particular make this very clear. This section of Matthew is called the "Parabolic Discourse." The Kingdom is Jesus' message. He never describes it conceptually; he walks around it and keeps giving images of the Real. This is the classic pattern of the spiritual teacher. Only those ready and seeking will normally understand. Others will read them as innocuous aphorisms. Scripture scholars in recent decades have broadened our understanding of these parables through their research into Jesus' times.

For example, "The kingdom of Heaven is like a mustard seed which a man took and sowed in his field. It is the smallest of all the seeds, but when it has grown it is the biggest of shrubs [which isn't really true] and becomes a tree, so that the birds of the air can come and shelter in its branches" (Matthew 13:31-32).

The mustard seed is very small and insignificant. Pliny the Elder, a contemporary of Jesus, wrote a great big book called *Natural History*, in which he describes all the plants that were known in the Mediterranean world. He says only two things about the mustard plant: It's medicinal, so it did have some value. But he said not to plant it because it tends to take over the entire garden. It is a weed that cannot be stopped.

Those would have been the two images that Jesus was clearly building on: What I'm describing for you is therapeutic—it's life, it's healing, it's medicinal—but it's like a weed. What a shocking image, like a virus: I'm planting a weed in the world. I'm going to talk about stupid things like nonviolence and simple life, but

40

they're planted and they're going to take over; the old world is over. I don't know if it's going to take two thousand years or four thousand years before you get the point, but I've planted what I know is eternal truth in the world and it's going to take over.

But there's opposition: the birds. We city folks picture the birds coming down into the branches, nice little bluebirds, won't that be nice. But birds to any farmer are a negative image: They eat up all your seeds! Birds are the enemy! Farmers don't want birds in their fields. So Jesus is saying, I'm planting something that's like a weed—a therapeutic one but a weed nonetheless. It's going to grow with great difficulty because there's going to be all kinds of opposition. But it will prevail; it will finally, eventually take over the whole garden.

That's Jesus' hope, but do you see what patient hope that is? He didn't see it happen in his lifetime. And remember, from the beginning Jesus proclaimed this Kingdom—the Real—in a world where ninety-eight percent of people were poor. They were all, except for the Romans, an occupied people. The vast majority of them were enslaved. Religion was highly corrupt. And still in the midst of that he dared to announce the present Reign of God! He dared to say, "You can live the new reality right now." Now that's most extraordinary.

The word for living that way, living in the in-between times, is *faith*. Get rid of every thought you've had about faith, if that's possible. Forget for the moment about believing in the Immaculate Conception or the pope. Those are fine, but they're not what Jesus is talking about. He's talking about the grace and the freedom to live God's dream for the world *now*—while not rejecting the world as it is. That's a mighty tension that is not easily resolved.

Remember this: There are always two worlds. The world as it operates is power; the world as it should be is love. The secret of Kingdom life is how can you live in both—*simultaneously*. The world as it is will always be built on power, ego and success. Yet we also must keep our eyes intently on the world as it should be—what Jesus calls the Reign of God. Power apart from love leads to brutality; but love that does not engage with power is mere sentimentality. A lot of Christians today are still trapped in one or the other.

Images of Hiddenness and Timing

Jesus told another parable right after the Mustard Seed: "The kingdom of Heaven is like the yeast a woman took and mixed in with three measures [about fifty pounds!] of flour till it was leavened all through" (Matthew 13:33b). If any of you have been to San Francisco and remember sourdough bread, you might have the correct image here. Leaven is not the nice little package you buy at the grocery store. That's our modern, sanitized version of what people have known for centuries as leaven.

Leaven actually evokes an image of corruption! (Thus the bread of the Passover had to be new and *un*leavened.) You set sourdough in the corner until it gets bubbly and smelly. Then Jesus says a woman took and hid this seemingly corrupt thing inside and it was enough to leaven, eventually, the entire fifty pounds! Clearly the three measures of flour is a deliberately large amount to give us hope.

Jesus is content, it seems, not to be the whole loaf but instead the smelly leaven that you put inside. That's who we are. And that's what you feel like when you start living the gospel—too full of leaven for anything else. Why don't I believe in all these other things? Why am I not excited about the elections? Every time we change presidents, people think it's going to make a big difference: Why can't I get excited about it? I have been salted, leavened and enlightened by a much bigger truth, that's why.

The point in the next two parables about the treasure and the pearl is the same.

> The kingdom of Heaven is like treasure hidden in a field which someone has found; he hides it again, goes off in his joy, sells everything he owns and buys the field.
> Again, the kingdom of Heaven is like a merchant looking for fine pearls; when he finds one of great value he goes and sells everything he owns and buys it. (Matthew 13:44-45)

The kingdom is hidden and yet available. God is perfectly hidden and perfectly revealed in every moment. The Kingdom is an open secret. Can you hold both of those words together? These are just flesh and blood people in my life, aren't they? These are just flowers? This is just a table, isn't it? God is perfectly hidden here, there is no way you see God! But God is perfectly revealed in every moment. Clearly this is an invitation to take this material world seriously. Physical creation is both the hiding place and the revealing place of God!

Matthew ends the Parabolic Discourse with Jesus asking, " 'Have you understood all these?' They said, 'Yes' " (13:51)—but it's so obvious they hadn't because we still haven't gotten the message two thousand years later! It's still hidden, subversive and not the way we want to see things.

The final verses of Chapter 13 are Matthew's signature: "Well then, every scribe who becomes a disciple of the kingdom of Heaven is like a householder who brings out from his storeroom new things as well as old" (13:51-52). We're not sure who really wrote this Gospel, but it probably was a converted scribe. Some scholars think this is his way of getting his name in there, and describing his task.

This scribe we call Matthew tried to bring out of the same storehouse things both new and old and put them together. That, I believe, is the work of the "magician," the work of spirituality, the work of Jesus. It creates a new symbolic universe at the dangerous level of imagination. Jesus is involved in a war of myths; the ultimate battle for the soul is to change the way we imagine our reality.

In the Parabolic Discourse, Jesus tells us to withdraw our allegiance from a world of bigness, clarity, immediacy, looking good and security (the old order) and to see life instead as smallness, patience, humility, inner wisdom and risk-taking (always new and rare).

Once your symbolic world changes, once you're converted in the guts, you're trapped in the truth and you can never forget it. You can no longer take some things seriously. The Sermon on the Mount—indeed all of the gospel—creates for you that new symbolic universe.

CHAPTER THREE

Finding the Jesus Who Preached the Sermon

We say "Jesus Christ" as if Christ is Jesus' last name. That's because we're so comfortable with putting the two identities together. You could say that Jesus in a certain sense is the historical man of Nazareth who walked this earth. And the Christ is the great archetypal identity that is put on Jesus once we have taken him to be our God-figure, the one who leads us to the Father. Both identities are true: Our faith as Christians is in Jesus Christ, the historical man Jesus *and* the cosmic Lord who is Christ.

In this book we're largely emphasizing Jesus, because until you get back to "Jesus before Christianity," as the Dominican Albert Nolan says, you just don't have anything solid to build on. You keep creating fantasy Jesuses—who can be molded to whomever we want Jesus to be. We've got to go back to the historical Jesus to rebuild our foundations. What did Jesus really teach and what are the later developments from the tradition and from the Church?

As we name how history and culture have shaped our understanding of Jesus, we've got to admit the biases of each century. What problems of the first century was Jesus addressing? Why did his contemporaries see Jesus in a certain way? Are the questions of Jesus the perennial human questions?

We moderns are coming along after two thousand years with accretion upon accretion—they can feel like barnacles on a ship! Will the true Jesus please stand up? Who is Jesus? There's been much exciting scholarship in recent years. We are learning to be honest about the historical Jesus, to let him speak for himself through the Scriptures.

Inspired Biases
Two Differing Pictures of Jesus

Synoptic Gospels (Matthew, Mark and Luke)	*The Gospel of John*
Start with John the Baptist, infancy stories, perhaps birth.	Starts with cosmic creation, no birth or infancy narrative.
Jesus speaks like a Semitic sage, in parables and pithy aphorisms.	Jesus speaks in long, dense, theological narratives.
Jesus is a lay teacher and holy man.	Jesus is a mystic philosopher.
Jesus is an exorcist.	Jesus performs no exorcisms.
The "Kingdom" or "Reign of God" is Jesus' constant theme.	Jesus is announcing himself in his major proclamations.
Mostly action and explanation of action; little self-analysis by Jesus.	Jesus has created an entire theology and justification for everything he is and does.
Jesus is unfailingly on the side of the poor, the oppressed and the outsider. They are often praised above the believers and the establishments.	Such themes are hardly mentioned here. In fact, "we" are good while "Jews" and unbelievers are bad.
Whole story is about one year of adult ministry.	Public ministry lasts three years.
Extended last supper, passion, death and resurrection accounts.	Foot-washing replaces story of bread and wine. Highly stylized theology of passion, death and resurrection.

It is to be hoped that this quick overview of the obvious helps us to see that we have had varied theologies about Jesus from the beginning. Both pictures presented here are accepted as "orthodox" and true presentations of the only Jesus we know: the historical and transcendent figure who formed the faith of these writers and these communities. This is the Living Jesus who wrote a living Bible.

There is no such thing as an *entirely objective* viewpoint on anything. Every viewpoint is a view from a point! Intelligent and faith-filled reading of inspired texts merely takes that point seriously so it can better understand what Jesus was trying to say *in that original context*. His story is also our story.

(See the *Dogmatic Constitution on Divine Revelation* of the Second Vatican Council, especially chapters 1-3.)

Modern Jesus Scholarship

Modern New Testament scholars are looking at the Gospels with new eyes, trying to piece together how much actually comes from the life of Jesus and how much is the interpretation of the early Church.

Almost none of John's Gospel is considered by mainstream scholars today to be directly from Jesus. Most of what Jesus says in John's Gospel are words put in Jesus' mouth by this community around the year 100 or 110. It is not corroborated by other Gospels or writings, to our knowledge. That doesn't make it wrong. The point in studying the New Testament is this: The story is *always true*—and sometimes it really happened! That is the nature of all sacred Scriptures.

The written Gospels are the unfolding of the story as those who loved and followed Jesus understood his words seventy or eighty years later. Those stories are presented by the faith communities— in their context, given their bias, given their problems and their needs. You can clearly see that's true by noting how the Gospels contradict one another. The Gospels are not presenting the historical Jesus, for the most part. But then again, they are not entirely ahistorical, either. Jesus was certainly real and historical, but as his story was told many decades after his death, filled with variety and interpretation.

47

If you're not willing to live with that, you've got nothing else to build on, because that's all we have: our reconstructions of narrative once or twice removed from the historical Jesus but grounded in the early Christian community. That demands of Christians a great act of faith in what we call inspiration or the guidance of the Holy Spirit. We believe that the Spirit was guiding this community as it developed and unfolded its belief in the historical Jesus. That's how we get from a peasant proclaiming the Kingdom of God in Galilee through mythic imagery to the year 100, where we have the divine Son of God walking around, calling himself by God's name, "I-AM-WHO-AM."

Only in John's Gospel does Jesus say "I AM." Jesus doesn't say it in Mark, Matthew or Luke. The faith there is still unfolding and finding appropriate words—as, indeed, it still is today.

Yet that doesn't mean John's Gospel isn't true. It means it tells what the Spirit in the Johannine community has come to recognize by the year 100. They have what we call a "high" or developed Christology. They have come to understand Jesus as the Christ— the Anointed One, as the Son of the Father and as the Divine Logos (Word of God).

Much of what is in the Gospels results from new situations and new problems encountered by the early Christian communities. The Jesus story was remembered and passed on verbally over a period of thirty to seventy years before the Gospels were written. This early preaching is called the *kerygma*. It was the first language used by believers to describe their faith experience of Jesus. For almost thirty years it was largely oral.

Put yourself in the sandals of an apostle. You're standing up there, you're presenting Jesus, you've got to make this Jesus fit this crowd and so you sort of embroider the words a little. That's certainly been the way of preachers throughout history, including this one! When I preach, I've got to make it so twentieth-century Americans coming from our background can understand Jesus. I put another level onto it. A preacher cannot *not* do that! There is no such thing as uninterpreted fact in the human world.

This adaptation of the Jesus story to address new situations comes from the pre-biblical Church. It may be unsettling to some, but the Church *did* exist before the Bible. The Church had a source of authority before it had the Bible: the Christian community itself, its belief, its oral tradition. That's what Catholics held onto for good and for ill. We believe there are, in fact, two fonts of revelation: Scripture *and* Tradition. There always have been two sources—and there is likely no other way.

Now when Martin Luther comes along in the 1500's, he says *sola scriptura*, "Scripture alone." Of course, Luther didn't admit his own biases. Luther had a whole bunch of tradition that he didn't realize he was carrying along with him. Since there is no such thing as a bias-free or value-free position, all we need to do is be aware of that bias in ourselves and others. Again, every viewpoint is a view from a point.

That's not to put down Luther; that's just to recognize you can't be *sola scriptura*. It's impossible. You necessarily come from a culture, from a temperament, from an economic worldview, a social worldview. Luther did, too. As much as he says he's only appealing to the authority of Scripture, it's obvious in hindsight that many of the things he chooses to notice in Scripture were responding to his own issues.

Please don't underestimate Luther's contribution, though. Many of the practices of the Roman Catholic Church were misguided, and Luther, priest and Bible scholar, correctly recognized that. Catholicism eventually dealt with them, although sometimes in a reactionary way, during the Counter-Reformation.

What Luther did with Scripture is what the Catholic hierarchy is doing, and what you're doing too, and that's OK. Anyone serious about understanding the New Testament has to get away from the way most of us were taught the Bible. We have to become a little more historically aware and self-critical, admitting that human beings wrote the Bible and human beings have been interpreting it for centuries! Isn't it even more wondrous to believe that inspiration is in *us*, too? The Spirit is guiding human history, not just the written words.

Saint Paul and Luther likely had similar personalities. So Luther goes to Paul to find what he needs because both of them are struggling with the same issue: I want to be a good boy and I can't. I want to be perfect and I can't. Ah, God loves me unconditionally— hallelujah! Luther jumps up and Paul jumps up—"God loves me unconditionally!" But then they make that the whole gospel; every emphasis of one point is necessarily a deemphasis of another.

They both miss almost everything Jesus says about social justice, and about all the other issues that most concerned Jesus himself. I don't mean to put down the experience of unconditional love; you have to have it, too, for all of this to make sense. But you can't just pump up people every Friday night by reconvincing them of God's unconditional love. Finally you've got to go out into the vineyards and marketplaces of the world and preach "good news to the nations" (see Matthew 28:19) and not just to individuals. Paul was, of course, doing this by his emphasis on community and Church order.

Beyond repeating actual sayings of Jesus and adapting these for early pastoral situations, the Gospels include much that seems to be an outright creation of new sayings and stories by the earliest Christian communities. In these new sayings and stories the communities document their understanding of Jesus. And in some cases, we must admit, the new context changes the content of Jesus' original message. They are clearly making a new point: Thus the same healing story will be remembered three or four different ways.

We try to trust that even those new points are good points for us because they were good points for Matthew's community in the year 90. For that is when Matthew's Gospel was put to papyrus: about sixty years after Jesus' death and resurrection. The self-criticism and self-congratulation that we find *in the final text* is, in fact, the exact kind of narrative that we need to encourage us to go and do likewise! That is also inspiration and probably the most helpful form of inspiration. It profits no one to say that only the historical event exactly as it happened is the source of divine guidance.

Three Sources for Matthew

Matthew's Gospel as we have it today was compiled in the early years of the Church from three sources. The first of the three sources is what we think of as Mark's Gospel. That Gospel could have been written as early as 60 but perhaps as late as 70.

Imagine the difference between 1956 and 1996. We're talking

about a generation or longer after Jesus' death and resurrection before we begin to get the first Gospel. That's why it's foolish ever to look upon the Gospels as biographies of Jesus. They're masterpieces of theology, of mythology in the best sense of that term, of history in the best sense of that term—but not our twentieth-century rational, scientific understanding of history.

The second source is often called the Q Document—Q for the German word *quelle*, meaning "source." We don't have this anymore, but we surmise that it must have existed. From careful study and comparison, we see that Matthew and Luke must draw upon some common source outside of themselves that we no longer have. That's the Q Document.

The third source is tradition and the perceptions of Matthew's communities—the problem he is trying to solve—and the oral fragments that have come down to them. This is sometimes called the M source.

With all of that said, we can look at how the Gospels were written. First we have stage one, the historical event itself, to which there are very few if any eyewitnesses (for example, Jesus and Satan in the desert). Yet the Gospels are not concerned with conveying an accurate biography of Jesus. That's our hangup. The Gospels are about telling the *meaning* of Jesus, and his effect on their lives. This is personal testimony, "good news" more than empirical facts.

Then we have stage two, very specific situations in each of the communities. The Synoptic Gospels (Matthew, Mark and Luke) look at things in somewhat the same way, with variations for these situations. (*Syn op* means "to see the same.") New Testament scholars compare the similar passages and identify how each passage was slightly changed. They look for what was included and what was left out. That reveals the biases. That's how we can assume for example, that Matthew was talking to a middle-class community and Luke was talking to a poor community: because we see the kinds of stories they'll skip, the kinds of phrases they'll add, the kinds of words they'll include or exclude. All of that reveals the bias or pastoral concern of each author.

The written Gospels as we have them come from a third stage, built upon the first and the second. They were composed by evangelists and their disciples according to the needs and understandings of their time and place, decades after the historical life of Jesus.

Yet the four Gospels can only be understood in relation to all three stages: the historical event, the way each of the early Christian communities interpreted it, how the final author wrote it down. Our act of faith—and it *is* an act of faith—is that all three stages are in fact divine revelation: God acting in history to reveal *who God is* and what happens when God encounters humanity. The text is a "text in travail" revealing the patterns and process itself, not just the conclusions. This is why Scripture is such a fruitful source of transformation for every age, but also very open to misuse by those who don't enter into the "travail" themselves.

For a believing Christian, both the life of the Word of God and the text of the word of God are illuminated by the process of historical reconstruction. Again, I want to say that I consider such a style of revelation an extra plus and not a deficiency. Now we can expect God's revelation in our history, too—not just back in the good old days.

Though it came from three sources, the Gospel of Matthew was not haphazardly written. The author clearly had a sense of outline, as most good writers today do. Matthew's Gospel is too well ordered not to have an underlying plan and intended audience. Our job is to accept his agenda, not to force Matthew into ours. Then we will have *teaching*.

First of all we have the two bookends: the Prologue and the Epilogue. The Prologue is what we call Chapter 1. (Chapter and verse numbers were not put in until the Middle Ages.) When Matthew wrote he didn't know that he was writing a book of the Bible. He was just writing the Good News for the Christian community.

Matthew differs from Mark. Mark's Gospel is basically an account of the passion, death and resurrection of Jesus. One gets the sense that all Mark's authors really cared about was revealing the great mystery of death and resurrection. They added some simple stories of healings and teachings up front, but the passion, death and resurrection is central. Jesus finally stops talking. He knows we're going to miss the point in words. We won't believe it unless he walks through it himself and says, "This is the way through: crucifixion and resurrection."

Rather than focus so much on the passion, death and resurrection of Jesus, Matthew composes a Gospel of five books. And each book is a combination of a series of narratives and sermons. The narrative, in most cases, prepares you for the sermon that follows.

Jesus' Worldview

The sermon that we're going to spend most time on is the inaugural sermon, the Sermon on the Mount (Matthew 5—7). Recent scholarship reaffirms that it is as close as we can get to Jesus' original teaching; it seems to be the heart of the teaching of the historical Jesus. It surely represents the style of a Jewish peasant layman: aphorisms, stories and parables that are provocative, quotable, often short and memorable. Very often they cut against the grain of conventional wisdom, while focusing on a God who is good and can be trusted.

Matthew's narratives are usually collections of healing stories, exorcisms and confrontations of growing hostility between Jesus and the establishment. All this finally builds to a kind of climax with the scene in the Temple that leads to Jesus' passion, death and raising up.

We've tended to soften Jesus' conflict with the system ever since we became a Church of the establishment. The year that we blame is the year 313. That is the year of the Edict of Milan or the Constantinian Revolution. It is then that the Church changed dramatically and changed sides dramatically. Up until that time the Church was by and large of the underclass. It identified with the oppressed and the poor; the Church itself was still being oppressed and Christians were being thrown to the lions. It reads history from the catacombs; literally from underground, which always gives you a different perspective than "those found in palaces"—exactly how Jesus distinguishes his cousin John (see Matthew 11:8).

Now Emperor Constantine thinks he's doing us a favor in 313 when he makes Christianity the established religion. Yet it might be the single most unfortunate thing that happened to Christianity.

Once we moved from the bottom of society to the top, we developed a new film over our eyes, and we couldn't read anything that showed Jesus in confrontation with the establishment. We *became* the establishment. Clear teaching on issues of greed, powerlessness, nonviolence, non-control and simplicity were moved to the sidelines, if not actually countermanded.

We'll see as we get into the Sermon on the Mount that Jesus intended for us to take the low road. He intended us to operate from the minority position, from the position of "immoral" minority much more than the moral majority. When you're protecting your self-image as a moral, superior or "saved" person, you always lose the truth. The daring search for God—the common character of all religion—is replaced with the search for personal certitude and control.

As long as the Church was underground in some sense, as long as we operated from a minority position, we had greater access to the truth, to the gospel, to Jesus. We in our time have to find our way to disestablish ourselves, to identify with our powerlessness instead of our power, our dependence instead of our independence, our communion instead of our individualism. Unless we understand that, the Sermon on the Mount isn't going to make any sense.

As soon as people are comfortable, they don't want any truth beyond their comfort zone. People who are at the top of the system normally will vote "conservative" because once you're at the top of a system you want to conserve the system as it is. You're enjoying its fruits; why would you want to change it? Yet those who are not enjoying the fruits of the system are always longing and thirsting for the coming of the Kingdom, for something more. They are not as likely to vote for the status quo, which is invariably built on those bottom lines of money, power and God-talk. For the millennial vision, the Messianic promise, life has to be more than this. The gospel always keeps us on that side of the question, in a state of longing and thirsting for God. Grace seems to create a void inside of us that only grace can fill.

I believe that Jesus is the great reconciler. Picture two lines, one line going vertically, one line going horizontally: That's the cross. Pioneer psychologist Carl Jung says Jesus was killed on the coincidence of opposites. Whenever you try to hold opposite energies together—liberal/conservative, masculine/feminine, right/wrong, black/white—anything that's conflictive, you're going to get crucified. When you see the cross, picture a collision of opposites, the coming together of opposing energies, both of which invariably think they're the whole truth.

Paul saw this clearly thirty years after Jesus died:

> ...God wanted all fullness to be found in him
> and through him to reconcile all things to him,
> everything in heaven and everything on earth,
> by making peace through his death on the cross.
> (Colossians 1:19-20)

Bridge-builders, including Jesus, usually start building a bridge from one side. You can't build a bridge from the middle, as even an engineer will tell you. You must choose a starting point. What the gospel is saying, pure and simple, is that wherever you're going to start building your bridge, you better start from the side of powerlessness, not power. Because if you start on the side of power you'll stay there forever. You really won't build any bridges.

Yet you can't stay on the side of powerlessness. You're going to discover the true meaning of power as you build the bridge over to it. And Jesus will redefine the nature of power for you. So we must be bridge-builders. We must pay the price in our body for building those bridges (see Colossians 1:24) and know we'll be abused and misquoted from both sides. But the necessary starting point for building the bridge of the gospel is from the side of powerlessness, either political powerlessness or your personal powerlessness, preferably both. And if you start there you have a good chance of coming to the truth. It will always be a conversion, a turning around, to get back to what some call "beginner's mind."

Let's put that in the back of our hearts and minds. Maybe it will set the stage for getting into the text. Let that prepare us to understand why Jesus is going to say such nonsensical, ridiculous things. Because powerlessness, as best I can read the Gospels, is the Kingdom worldview of Jesus. Without emptiness, there can be no fullness; without a beginner's curiosity, there can be no learning. Only those who possess nothing can be entrusted with everything.

We saw in the first two chapters of this book that Jesus of

Nazareth challenged his disciples to accept an entirely new system of values, a new world order. In this chapter, I hope, I have explained what some of those values are. In the remainder of this book, we will be reading the Bible in perhaps a new way. Now we will turn to a detailed look at the society Jesus was challenging, and an explanation of why Matthew tells the story the way he does.

CHAPTER FOUR

Understanding the Social Order

M ost societies create classes consciously or unconsciously. Like it or not, it gives great comfort to the psyche at least to know where you stand. Societies with obvious classes tend to create less widespread discontent than societies like ours, which falsely claims not to have classes.

People tend to compare themselves with other people within their class. Workers tend to compare themselves to other workers, intellectuals to other intellectuals, and so on. *Our* worldview, however, tends to lend itself to across-the-board envy, competition and comparison. Many of us go through life preoccupied with the hope of moving into a higher class. We have the illusion we could make tons of money if only we were smart or lucky enough.

No wonder so many people in our society are anxious! The ego only knows itself by comparisons. And comparing is a losing game: Our reference points are always changing. We are building on sand.

To understand the social order Jesus was challenging, one must understand the class system of agrarian society. At the outset, I would like to express my indebtedness to John Dominic Crossan and his book *The Historical Jesus: The Life of a Mediterranean Jewish Peasant* (HarperCollins, 1991) for his rendition of much of the scholarship that follows. Please do not construe my use of Crossan's valuable scholarship on the life and times of Jesus as any kind of endorsement of his ultimate conclusions, which drew fire from many critics. I am not relying on his conclusions in this book; only on his accurate picture of Jesus' culture.

During Jesus' time, most of the world lived in agrarian societies. Gerhard E. Lenski, in his 1966 book *Power and*

Privilege: A Theory of Social Stratification (New York: McGraw-Hill) identifies nine classes of agrarian society. At the top of society was the ruler. The ruler is one person in a class alone, usually the king or queen. In most agrarian societies, the ruler controlled or had complete access to at least twenty-five—and often fifty—percent of the gross national product. Everything went to aggrandizing that person.

From our perspective we can ask, "Wasn't that evil?" But underneath the enormous inequity there were actually some positive aspects. Without condoning it too much, we can say having a ruling class gave people much more social security in the real meaning of that term than people have now. People knew where they stood, what their role was.

In a more rigid class society, you don't compare yourself to the ruler: He's the ruler, he's in that class, he's *supposed* to have the lion's share of the gross national product. People outside the ruling class accept what they have.

The second class in agrarian society—about one percent—was the governing class: the bureaucrats, nobles and officials who surrounded the ruler. They received as a group at least an additional twenty-five percent of the gross national product. This one percent and the ruler, then, owned at least half and often seventy-five percent of all the goods and services in the society.

Then there was the retainer class, those who maintain the system. These were lower-class bureaucrats: the military, scribes and teachers in Jesus' society. They comprised about five percent of the population. Retainers serve the political elite. They are the secretaries and soldiers who want to keep their jobs. So they fight for the ruler and the one percent who have the money. Retainers have some degree of education and know-how.

The retainer class in Jesus' society merits a closer look before we examine the other classes. The scribes were in that class. You may have noticed in so many of the miracle stories and the exorcisms, the scribes are upset with Jesus. Why? Because he is taking away their job security. If you want to see the import of any of Jesus' miracles, read who he's talking to at the beginning and who's upset at the end.

Normally the people who are upset at the end have just seen

their job made unnecessary. Scribes, equivalent to lawyers today, were those who had manufactured, since the days of Leviticus and Numbers, very complex systems of laws that created a demand for their expertise. Scribes helped people to wade through the system. And of course to wade through with them you had to pay them a little bit.

In Israel at the time of Jesus, Church and state were one; the laws were largely tied up with religion. For example, there were very clear rules of how a person with leprosy is to be made clean and what the person must do. There were clear rules about how a woman must be treated. So when Jesus goes walking around the countryside touching people saying "Be made clean!" that's a subversive action. "You can't do this!" a scribe might have said. "You've just ignored the whole legal system" (read: "You've just taken away our benefits!").

With that in mind, it might be more obvious why most of the Jewish leadership cooperated in having Jesus killed. Jesus was making God too accessible. He ignored the debt codes, the purity codes and the honor-and-shame system which held the whole thing together. We'll take a closer look at that toward the end of this chapter.

The governing class, retainers and rulers were, of course, almost entirely against Jesus—with some precious and beautiful exceptions. Matthew, for example, describes himself as a former scribe who is converted, which is why he understands the message so well. He was a man of the system.

The merchant class comes next. That was very small in agrarian society. In Jesus' lifetime, it was certainly less than five percent. It wasn't until the time of Saint Francis, the thirteenth century, that the merchant class began to take over. Today, merchants control the world! But a dominant merchant class is a new phenomenon, as is an industrial society based on consuming and producing. Since the beginning, most people on this earth have been farmers.

The last of the five classes who comprise the establishment was the priestly class. They were landowners then, just as they have been in one way or another throughout history. We'll zoom up fifteen centuries for a quick look at the situation at the Reformation to illustrate the point.

At the time of the Reformation religious orders owned more than half of Europe. The serfs worked for the monks. (I can understand why my father Saint Francis forbade Franciscans to own land. For some reason the religious establishment always gets into real estate.) The Reformation was more about politics than theology. It happened because of the moral and economic corruption of so much of the Church and because the Church owned so much land. The priestly class was tied up with land and buildings in Jesus' time too.

Besides the five ruling classes in agrarian society, there were lower classes. They comprised at least eighty percent of the society. Those who farmed the land were the peasant class. Very often they were tenant farmers—someone else owned the land. That's why so many of the parables of Jesus are about landlords and tenants. The folks he talked to could lose their land in a moment. They were at the whim of the ruling class and the landlords. *Two-thirds* of what they produced was spent on rent, taxes and tolls!

Imagine surviving as a peasant in a year of drought. After you've given two thirds away to the ruling class and to those to whom you're subservient (as if that isn't bad enough), you still have to save enough of your grain for seed for next year so you can plant again. And of course you have to save enough to feed your cattle or other livestock. Whatever tiny bit is left you and your children have to live on for a year. That's how most poor people have lived since the beginning of time. In the Third World today it is still much that way.

Jesus came from this lower group. He was a Galilean peasant. Some new studies even question whether Jesus was literate. Jesus was a poor, simple man who knew how peasants struggled. We must understand that to understand his message more fully. Most to whom he talked were people in the same situation. Jesus and his audience understood each other.

Within the peasant class there were subclasses. One, our seventh class, was the artisans. They, about five percent, were skilled workers, such as carpenters, who were recruited from the ranks of dispossessed peasants. They always had to depend upon a patron. The artisans were gifted, yet they remained poor.

The eighth class was the people deemed unclean by reason of

origin or of occupation. For example, in Jewish society people who took care of pigs were considered unclean. The "unclean" still exist in all societies today, although the label is more subtle and often unadmitted. (Poor people, people of color, gays and lesbians, old people, people with disabilities, non-Christians, foreigners—all these are the modern version of the unclean in Western society.) Jesus has a great deal of contact with this group.

But the unclean were not so low as the totally expendable class. That ninth class might have been as much as much as five to ten percent of all peasants: These expendable ones had to live by their wits. Call them criminals, or if they live at the charity of others, call them beggars. They are the unemployed or the unemployable. Lepers were often in this class, although sometimes they'd be a notch higher, in the unclean class.

The word Matthew uses for the poor in spirit, for example, at the beginning of the Sermon on the Mount, is *ptochoi*. It refers not just to peasants, but to these very bottom classes, the destitute. Jesus is saying, You're at the very bottom of the heap but I want you to know you've got freedom there and we're going to find it. And I'm going to help you find it. He's talking to the least of the brothers and sisters, as we will see in Matthew 25, the lowest of the peasant class. Many of Jesus' comments about the poor are about these last two classes, the unclean and the expendable people. The farmer still has his land. He's dirt poor but he at least has something to fall back on.

Before moving on, we should note a sad connection to our own society: At the close of the twentieth century, it's that final class which is growing so quickly, the expendable people who are unemployed and unemployable. There's no way we need you, we say, in effect. We will undereducate you, undertrain you and undervalue you. We even hope you kill one another. We hope the drugs and guns will allow you to kill one another because we can't fit you into our definition of success, our definition of reality. Yet it was the bottom of society that Jesus most consistently showed concern for. They seem to be the measure of how well we understand the new world order.

Who Is Your Patron?

The society of Jesus' day is also called a society of patronage. This kind of society has lasted in Mexico, for example, to a high degree even to our day. It's one of the reasons for conflict between Mexico and the United States. In a society of patronage you are not defined by what you have or what you know but *who* you know. Everything depends on your connections: If you don't have connections you just don't get anywhere.

That's why many of us will feel so lost, for example, if we go to Mexico: We have no connections there. One is powerless without connections. That's patronage society, and it's not just Mexico, but many societies. Most of the Mediterranean world was that way, and the cultures founded by the Mediterranean world still are. Italian and Spanish society retain patronage to some degree, although northern European society has lost it.

Older Catholics may understand this idea easily. The idea of the patron saint came out of the Mediterranean world. In a patronage society someone has to stand between the individual and the overlord. The patron saint is the same idea.

My community, the Franciscans, has been working with the Native Americans in the pueblos of New Mexico for centuries. Yet one of the things we haven't been able to change is the position of Jesus in the grand scheme of things. Jesus in the hierarchy is third, at best. First is the Great Spirit, God. Then comes the patron saint! That's why we have the big dances on the feast days of the patron saint. It's the pueblo's individual connection with the Big One. And Santa Clara, San Ildephonso, Santo Domingo (to name a few examples) is on your side. We older Catholics all had a patron saint who was up there batting for us, who was our connection.

When you've grown up as a peasant in a society of patronage, you're nothing. You're insignificant and you've got to get your connections, your patron. The loyalty in both directions is often admirable, and need not be judged merely by our supposed democratic standards.

That relationship of little person to patron—wherever it shows up in history—grows inevitably into a system of honor and shame. The little person must show honor and respect to the patron. And the patron has a moral obligation to take care of the little one who pays honor. There are obligations on both sides. In the West this became the feudal system that lasted for centuries.

We don't really understand that system anymore. We have immediate access, we don't need patrons. Protestantism embraces patronless theology because it in many ways was a reaction against corrupt feudal institutions. Protestants as a whole don't understand Mary or the saints; Protestantism doesn't want any go-betweens.

Jesus himself is the go-between, though, for all who call themselves Christian. That's the Christ image who stands as our mediating symbol between us and God. Jesus says "No one can come to the Father except through me" (John 14:6b). "Look at me and you'll know what God is like." Jesus is in effect our Great Patron who stands between us and God. He tells us we can trust God because God is like him. "Anyone who has seen me has seen the Father" (John 14:9b). Daringly he says, "I am the gate..." (John 10:7b).

All of that is background for understanding the Sermon on the Mount. Until you understand patronage society you won't understand a lot of the Sermon on the Mount or much of the rest of Jesus' teaching. In many ways, Jesus is taking away the broker that society established; he's telling the people that God is totally accessible, that God is available in reality itself, in experience itself, in the world of graced relationships. The Kingdom of God is in your midst (see Luke 17:21). You don't need to go through the brokerage system in Jerusalem or worship the emperor in Rome. What a threat to the system!

The system responded by killing him.

We've grown up with the imagery of John the Baptist shouting in the wilderness and bringing crowds of people to the Jordan River, pouring water over them for the forgiveness of sin. But do you realize what he's saying? In Jerusalem there was a watertight system for getting into the Temple and getting your sins forgiven, for getting worthy, for declaring who's in and who's out. Now we have this joker out in the desert just saying God is as available *as water* and "God can raise up children of Abraham from these very stones" (see Matthew 3:8). No wonder the religious establishment wanted him dead! (We'll take a closer look at John in Chapter Six of this book.)

It is significant that Jesus went out to be baptized by John. Jesus is accepting the new world order that John the Baptist is pointing to! Yes, he says, God is as available as water in the river.

A Look From the Bottom

The historian Thomas Carney wrote in *The Shape of the Past: Models and Antiquity* (Lawrence, Kan.: Coronado Press, 1975): "The voices that speak to us from antiquity are overwhelmingly those of the cultured few, the elites. The modern voices that carry on their tale are overwhelmingly those of white, middle-class, European and North American males." And that is true: Most of the history that we have is from less than two percent of the human population. Ninety-eight percent of the people who ever lived on this planet have been poor and uneducated.

Poor people didn't have the luxury of writing their history, to tell us what it was like to be persecuted, oppressed or simply used to build a pyramid. We hear about pyramid-building from the side of the Pharaohs who planned the pyramids—not the hundreds of thousands of people who had to give their lives to build them.

We've missed most of the story of history. That's a new insight for many people in the modern age. Yet there are some exceptions, and the Bible is one of them. It's exciting to consider that the Bible is resistance literature. With the exception of Leviticus and Numbers, written by the priestly classes, most of the Bible is written by or about people who are occupied, enslaved, poor or disenfranchised in some way!

In the Bible, we have a narrative from the bottom instead of from the top. And it endured, remarkably when you consider that few of the books in the Bible were written at first but handed down orally. Besides, who wants to hear about life from the side of a slave, a woman or a poor person? Even the New Testament reveals the remaining bias when it ends the multiplication stories with the telling phrase "to say nothing of women and children" (Matthew 14:21). Exactly. "The scholarship of antiquity is often removed from the real world," says Carney, "hygienically free of value judgments."

64

The same is true in our own country today. Every year we celebrate the Fourth of July and celebrate the heart-fluttering mythology that our founders loved freedom. Yet today we must acknowledge what they really meant when they said all "men" are created equal. The Declaration of Independence was written by rich white male landowners and it was talking about the enfranchisement of rich white males. The mythology of private property, guns and violence, racism and sexism is at the very foundation of our country.

American schoolchildren could easily get the idea that Jefferson's Declaration was a revolutionary document that empowered everyone to vote. Yet women weren't allowed to vote. And certainly blacks were not; they weren't even counted as full persons in the census! The lie was that we *believed* that we believed all people were created equal! What made us think we were this great free society? Those at the top believed it then, and we at the top believe it two hundred years later. That's the power of myth.

The Diversity of Human Experience

Where I live in New Mexico pilgrimages and images are more popular than sermons. Religion must express itself with music, dance and art. Western Christianity has probably been very limited because it has been run mostly by the educated clergy. Yet many will not be led to God by a sermon or a book, by well-formulated theology or even logic.

This doesn't mean that they are less smart; only that they come to reality in a different way, by intuitive leaps. My own father, for example, was a Kansas farmer. When he and Mom used to come and listen to me talk, my mother would just sit there, absorbed in my words, as many mothers might be. But Dad would fall asleep about ten minutes into it. But he didn't want to sleep through my talk. So he'd wake up and ask Mother, "Where does he get all those ideas?" And in effect he was saying, Why do we need all of those ideas? Perhaps he was right.

If you're not a big idea person, trust that your way of naming reality works and is fine.

Indians in New Mexico dance, for example. Their dance is their prayer. Then Christians come along and say, that's secular. Yet why would giving your thoughts to God please God more than giving your body to God? It's just that we're biased in favor of the mind, thinking the mind is the supreme faculty. That's not necessarily so! It's the bias of the elite, who often are overeducated in the head. Body, heart, gut people come to God in different ways than through correct or interesting ideas.

My point here is that the gospel is not primarily a set of facts but a *way of seeing and a way of being in the world because of God.* Jesus speaks to the heart, saying (1) God is on your side; (2) God can be trusted; (3) the universe is safe and benevolent; (4) trust yourselves, one another and God; (5) there is no reason to be afraid; (6) it's all heading toward something good! He does this primarily by touch, relationship, healing and parables.

Jesus Is Pro-Feminine

In the Gospels, Jesus goes out of his way to honor the feminine viewpoint. In fact, he represents it in much of his own life. This is why most feminists don't criticize Jesus; they criticize Christianity, and rightly so! Jesus, in terms of sexism, is a man well ahead of his time, and his attitude is so out-of-culture that one could almost use it as an argument for his divine Sonship.

In the story of the woman at the well (John 4:1-42), for example, Jesus breaks all the taboos by talking to a woman in public. By giving her credence, letting her talk back to him, ignoring the upset of his disciples, he violates the established codes of conduct. He knows they have no meaning in light of eternal values. Once Jesus meets eternal values he just lets go of relative cultural values. He knows that they do not bind him.

The one story where it might seem that Jesus is dismissive and derogatory toward a pagan woman, telling her it is not fair to toss the children's (Israel's) food to the dogs (Mark 7:24-30 or Matthew 15:21-28), turns out to be exactly the opposite. He initially seems to reflect the cultural, male or religious prejudice toward her, but then accepts her rejoinder, admits he is wrong, praises her—and apologizes by healing her daughter! This is a perfect morality play of prejudice and patriarchy *overcome.*

Jesus truly was dangerous: He was creating a following with a kind of thinking that was much more on the side of inclusiveness than exclusiveness. That tension between exclusiveness and inclusiveness is one of the central themes of Jesus' ministry.

Jesus is always moving the boundaries out while still respecting the center. That's the key to wisdom: being grounded in the center and still, from that deep foundation, knowing how to move out. Remember Archimedes, the Greek who said, "Give me a lever and a place to stand and I can move the world." What Jesus had—and what we need—is a place to stand. The ground on which he stood was his experience of God. His lever was what we call the gospel.

The danger of post-modern liberal society is that most people have no place to stand. Post-modern life is like a movable feast (or famine!): Everything is relative, in question and in constant motion. Jesus will give his followers a clear place to stand—the tradition of Judaism—but he reinterprets the tradition. He moves the boundaries out from a stable and secure center.

Changing the Boundaries

We will see in the teaching of Jesus and his Sermon on the Mount in particular that Jesus critiques and reorders the values of his culture from the bottom up. He "betrays" the prevailing institutions of family, religion, power and controlling of resources by his loyalty to another world vision, which he calls the Reign of God. Such loyalty cost him general popularity, the support of the authorities, immense inner agony and finally his own life. By putting the picture in the largest possible frame, he called into question all smaller frames and forced a radical transformation of consciousness upon his hearers. Many were not ready for it.

In Jesus' world of the first century, the dominant institution was the kinship system: the family, the private home. That's why first-century Christian Churches were house Churches. They were nothing like what you would call your parish. We're talking about small gatherings in private homes.

In Matthew's Gospel the word *house* is used many times. Jesus is always going in and out of houses. And, like today, what happened around the tables in those houses both shaped and named the social order. That is the key to understanding the power Jesus exercised at table. That might be Jesus' most significant social demonstration, a social action with subversive consequences. The power and meaning of table fellowship in Jesus' life probably is why the Eucharist stayed on, especially in the Catholic tradition, as the central symbol. The Eucharist builds upon Jesus' tradition of eating in a new way. We'll examine that more closely in the next chapter of this book.

Economics and the Western World

In our social setup family isn't first—as we are becoming painfully aware—nor is religion, nor even politics. What drives the institutions (government, social policy and the like) in our culture is *money*. Some people say politics is the driving institution, but people often are naive politically, ignorant of the power and reality of politics.

The dominant institution in our society is the system of production and consumption. The central value of our culture is buying and selling. It pervades everything. When you go to movies there are advertisements at the beginning of the movie that you paid six bucks to see! Commercialism is invading everything because the entire system is built on the commandments, "Thou shalt produce" and "Thou shalt consume."

Sometimes I turn on the TV talk shows when I'm reading my mail. It's a window into how Middle America thinks. I saw one recently that featured "freeloaders"—people who live off their grandmother or whomever. The wrath from the studio audience toward these people was uncanny! It was not just that they were taking advantage of someone's generosity. It was as if the freeloaders had broken the ultimate taboo: They were not producers. And several of them were saying they live on almost nothing and that's why they can do it. That meant they were breaking a double taboo: They weren't consuming either!

I'll bet you've heard your friends talk this way, as if to consume is a religious act. How did we turn reality around to make consumption and buying a virtue? If you listen to peoples' conversation you can hear it. You might hear someone say, "I bought a new car even though my old one worked fine. It's good for the economy." It could only happen in a culture where economics is the number one institution and the other three (family, religion and politics) are subservient to it.

The form of authority in our culture is not patriarchy as it would be in most kinship societies. (That probably explains some of our problem with priesthood and the papacy.) The father figure symbolically holds the family together (but even that is changing as fewer families have resident fathers). It is not religious ideology as in a religious culture, or party authority, as in a political culture. Quite simply, it is wealth. Status in our society is attained by having money and the freedom to use it.

Religion in an Economic Culture

There have been cultures where the religious meaning dominates. Medieval Christendom agreed upon a primary meaning of God and the Christian religion in Europe. That doesn't mean they really lived it out or that all the structures were Christian, but there was an agreed-upon meaning system. Today we have the same in the Islamic states, and it's scaring us to death. Religion as the primary institution has more power to gather people than anything else because religion speaks to the depth of the soul. Islam is again a force to be dealt with in the world because it still has what we once had in the twelfth century: the culture held together by the power of the image of God.

When the economic institution is our primary lens, religion tends to be diluted by pragmatic, win/lose and power attitudes. God is bought and sold more than loved, waited for or surrendered to. Those of us from economic cultures need to meditate hard and long about why Jesus' one clear act of anger was aimed at those selling and buying in the Temple (see Matthew 21:12).

I once saw a cartoon in the *New Yorker* depicting a pedestal with a dollar bill enthroned on it. All the people around are bowing down. One person who is bowing down says, "The reason I like this religion is that at least we're not hypocritical." We Americans have this dangerous illusion that we're a religious people. Yet it's evident to anybody who can see that God is not on the pedestal here. Clearly our consumer system is on the pedestal and everything else is subservient: market morality, marketing of politicians, families revolving around mass consumption.

I once was teaching a class that was to be attended by a recently converted wealthy banker. I had been warned that he probably would take me to task for my criticism of the American Way, so I was prepared for the worst. I watched him during my talk, the man in the three-piece suit listening attentively, occasionally becoming stiff-shouldered. And sure enough, at break time he headed right for my podium.

Here it comes, I thought, the lecture on the "bottom line" that I hear from time to time from upset businessmen. "Father," he said, putting his hands on my shoulders, "I've got something to tell you. Not only is what you said true, but it's much truer then you even imagine." Then he explained to me a study documenting that the United States government's savings and loan bailout of 1989 was the biggest transfer of money from the poor to the rich in human history.

"But there's really no one to blame," he added, in spite of the visible few who went to jail for their corrupt actions. The whole system is skewed to protect those at the top at all costs, he said. In fact, I added, it's to protect the system itself, because the system is our goal. We abhor and denigrate welfare for the poor, but hardly blink at welfare for corporations or for the banking and military systems.

Those of us who were working in social service agencies before the Persian Gulf War will remember how tight money was for education programs, health care, libraries or almost any social institution. Washington always said they were out of money—even money for the infrastructure, like rebuilding bridges. These were called "special interests." Then suddenly we had billions of dollars to fight the Persian Gulf War to protect our oil and wealthy Kuwait. How did we get it overnight? Because it's always there to protect the system itself. That *is* the system: militarism and money. These are not special interests in an economic culture: They are prevailing common interest.

Honor and Shame: Then and Now

In a kinship society like Jesus', status was achieved through the honor/shame system. Therein lies the key to many of Jesus' examples. In the honor/shame system, you gain status, self-image and meaning primarily through how others see you. The system around Jesus didn't ask the individual to think in terms of "who I really am before God" (as Jesus did), or "what I feel about myself" (our culture), but rather, "How does my village see me?" Tribal cultures to this day are built on some kind of honor/shame system. That's how most societies operated before they become highly urbanized and industrialized. Your meaning is almost entirely tied up in how your family and friends see you. It gives great comfort to the ego, and it also gives great power for social control.

Japan is a modern example of a kinship system (that is only recently changing to an economic system), where the old honor/shame system still operates. When I was preaching in Japan I picked up two young men from New Jerusalem whom we'd sent to work with the poor in the Philippines. (I once was pastor of a charismatic community called New Jerusalem. Over the years, the community grew to the point where it sent some missionaries overseas.) These two missionaries had expensive cameras with them when we stopped to see the Hiroshima museum. Yet a sign said cameras were prohibited. The Japanese man who was showing us around said, "Just leave them here on the curb and we'll pick them up when we get back out." There were thousands of people walking by in all directions!

My two friends were anxious, but our guide assured us the cameras would be untouched. "We just don't steal, you know." Then he said if the cameras were stolen, he'd buy them new ones. They left their two expensive cameras on the curb at Hiroshima, we went into the museum, walked all the way through. When we got up to the second floor, my friend Michael looked out the window and there the cameras were, with Japanese walking all around them! An hour and a half later we returned to find the cameras untouched. It made me wonder why some call the United States a Christian nation and think of the Japanese as "pagans." The honor/shame system is largely gone for us. It is a stronger enforcer of morals than mere religious commandments.

It should be obvious: For new wine we will have to have new wineskins. Until you have new wineskins—a new social order—it doesn't make a bit of difference to teach people "Thou shalt not steal" and "Thou shalt not be greedy." Our system is set up on the assumption that greed at the top will "trickle down" to the poor on the bottom. President Ronald Reagan was the first one to put it so bluntly, but that's been the system all along. It doesn't change much from one ruler to the next. The gospel gives us the ability to stand outside of our own institutions and to see them with clarity.

In New Testament times, shame and honor were in fact moral values that people felt compelled to follow. If a situation called for retaliation, you had to retaliate. Not to retaliate would have been immoral, because you would have abandoned your honor. You were bound to be true to the honor of your village, your family, your self. For Jesus to walk into the midst of that and say, "Do not retaliate" was to subvert the whole honor/shame system.

Once challenged, Jesus' listeners were given a new place to find their identity: in God. Who you are in God is who you are. That's the end of ups and downs. My value no longer depends upon whether my family or village likes me, whether I'm good-looking, wealthy or obedient to the laws. Jesus' message is incredibly subversive in an honor/shame society! Yet as he takes away their old foundations, he offers a new, more solid one: neither shame-nor guilt-based, but based in who-you-are-in-God.

Saint Francis said the same thing to his society: Who I am is who I am in God, nothing more, nothing less. And although that might sound scary at first, it actually is good news. Who you are in God is a beloved daughter or a beloved son; you are no longer dependent on culture's or even your own estimation. Through your prayer, your awareness of God within you, you continually discover your true identity: "[T]he life you have is hidden with Christ in God" (Colossians 3:3b).

Honor is the opposite of what prayer teaches the heart. It is the value of a person in one's own eyes, or through the eyes of others. Honor is excellence as recognized by society, and therefore self-image and human value are forever shaky, changing, unreliable.

To counter such externalization, Jesus promotes the three great religious disciplines found in all of the great world religions: prayer, almsgiving and fasting. These are the three time-tested ways to get free from the false self. Yet Jesus adds a twist: In all three cases, he says, do it secretly. Why? Because by doing these practices away from others' eyes, you break your enmeshment in other people's image of you. You find your identity within yourself and in a transcendent reference point.

I am glad we coined the word *codependency*! Even if we overuse the term, we've named why most people don't have a very solid self-image. For some, it's entirely based on what their spouse thinks of them—and when their spouse dies, they die. It's almost as if I'm no one apart from what my husband, wife or children or others think of me—which must be monitored, assessed and controlled day by day. What basic insecurity the modern world finds itself in!

Without the spiritual journey we're all enmeshed, even if we're not in a kinship-based society. Without the contemplative journey into true self, we are who our neighbor says we are. We fall deeper into this fragile self as we preoccupy ourselves with celebrities, soap operas and the cults of public figures. Infotainment takes the place of documentary; images take the place of substance.

How many can live up to society's standards of worth: good looking, blonde, slim, making money, a part of the jet-set? Surely no more than five percent of people can live up to these images. All the rest of us, in some way, feel inadequate, stupid and ugly. That's why teen suicide is at an all-time high, why every social indicator indicates that we are a culture massively deteriorating. Our cultural standards for success are more narrow than religion's ever were! And the result is widespread feelings of inadequacy.

This is an issue for women and men in our culture. Women especially are expected to live up to an impossible ideal for most of them in terms of youthful looks, slim figures, body proportions. It can be an uphill struggle to maintain self-esteem if you don't fit the mold. Men, too, tend to define their worth in terms of outside factors like appearance, power and job status. Economic cultures tend to produce more and more men who are unacceptable and outsiders to the system of success. No wonder that California alone is building twelve more prisons.

When I was in the hermitage I faced this at a level that surprised me. I was ashamed to admit it to myself. When I got away from the crowds who always listen to my preaching and feed my ego, I was at a bit of a loss. At a really deep level I felt a fear of insignificance, of being nothing.

When I saw that within myself I wept. I saw myself over the years trying to prove myself, somehow, and finding my self-worth in my success as an evangelist. I saw within myself a false motive for much of my work—and I was ashamed before God of what I saw. Yet I think that motive of proving ourselves is in all of us. Each of us carries that terrible fear that we are nothing. Among the five billion of us on this planet, how could God notice me?

Every town has the hard-to-get-to spot where the teens paint graffiti, late at night, at tremendous risk. Yet when the soul feels utterly insignificant, it writes its name where you can't miss it.

I once visited our lay missionaries from the New Jerusalem Community who were working in Saint Lucia, a little Caribbean island. A student at a local high school told me, "Father, do you know that our island isn't even on some maps of the world?" And we think *we* feel insignificant! Almost everyone there is too poor ever to move anywhere else. Imagine if your little dot, the only world you'll ever know, isn't even on the map. Without God, without being tied to the eternal, the soul collapses into insignificance. The tendency is to hand over our momentary significance to other people's estimation of us. That's an honor/shame society. Do you see the genius of advising such folks to pray, fast and give alms *in secret*? Jesus calls them to interiority, to find their validation in God alone.

Only prayer lets you realize that who you are is who you were in God before anybody thought anything: before you thought about whether you are good or bad, before anybody else thought about whether you are good or bad. You came forth from God and you will return to God. You are eternal. That's the only solid ground. That's the rock of the spiritual journey. That's what Jesus means when he says in Luke's Gospel that "your names are written in heaven" (10:20b). You're an eternal creation of God and there's no point in denying it or trying to dress it up; it already is. That's the ultimate good news.

But the good side of an honor/shame system is that it makes communities much more possible. It creates a world of interdependent people who rely upon one another, who stick together, who understand loyalty and commitment. We don't have that anymore because we're all largely trying to define our image through media images not really tied up with our identification as brother, sister, family. Thus we see community collapsing. It's very hard to create community or to create cooperation in such a world. That's a difference between our times and New Testament times: Jesus preached in a world where community was still understood, where an appropriate sense of honor and shame kept people bound and loyal to their commitments and to one another.

We live in a world where honor and shame are merely manipulated month by month by TV, tabloids, fashion magazines, commercials and now even by the marketing of politics and court cases. It seems like every eight months the moral issue that we should feel shame or outrage about changes: sexual harassment, crime, teen pregnancy, pedophilia, the deficit, family violence, abortion and so on. We cannot build a community of values unless we are a part of something more solid and enduring—where appropriate honor and shame reflect perennial human qualities to which we are locally accountable.

As we will see in the next chapter, the meal became Jesus' model for such teaching.

CHAPTER FIVE

Table Fellowship in the New Testament

Jesus didn't want his community to have a social ethic; he wanted it to *be* a social ethic. Their very way of relating was to be an affront to the system of dominance and power; it was to name reality in a new way. They were to live in a new symbolic universe. This radical idea is given in a simple clue found throughout the New Testament, a clue biblical scholars overlooked until only recently: Jesus' presence with others at table. That theme is so constant in the New Testament that scholars today see it as central to Jesus' message.

I'm no scholar, but I have a tremendous respect for what scholars do. After wading through the footnotes of a number of recent studies on the historical Jesus, I hope to be able to share in plain language what I've discovered. You may be as surprised as I was that we didn't see it all along.

In *The Historical Jesus*, New Testament scholar John Dominic Crossan writes of Jesus:

> He tells the missionaries not to carry a bag because they do not beg for alms or food or clothing or anything else and they do not carry bread. They share a miracle and a kingdom and they receive in return a table and a house.

Here I think is the heart of the original "Jesus Movement." That's an expression the scholars use and I think it's a good one. Calling the original gathering the Jesus Movement helps us avoid getting concerned with Church language too early. We need to understand the Jesus Movement before we can understand its later evolution into a Church.

There is a shared egalitarianism of spiritual and material resources among Jesus' followers. I want to emphasize this as strongly as possible and I insist that its facticity and symbolism cannot be separated. The mission we are talking about is not like Paul's, a dramatic thrust along major trade routes to urban centers hundreds of miles apart. Yet it concerns the longest journey in the Greco-Roman world, maybe in any world: the step across the threshold of a peasant stranger's home.

Shared home and common meal must be understood against the cross-cultural anthology of food and commensalism [table fellowship]. It is owing precisely to the complex interaction of cultural categories that food is commonly one of the principal ways in which differences among social groups are marked.

Crossan goes on to describe an anthropologist's research of many studies, with the conclusion that in all cultures, sharing food is a complex interaction that symbolizes group relationships and defines group boundaries almost more than any daily event.

No doubt you have become more aware of this if you've ever spent any time with a group of new acquaintances away from home. We experienced it constantly at our guest house for interns at the Center for Action and Contemplation in New Mexico. Groups of interns come and live in our guest house for months at a time. Over the years, there probably has been no single issue that brought up more feelings and discussion than food. A tremendous amount of time is put into what we buy, how much we pay for it, who gets it, who fixes it, how much is fixed, with what quality, and who cleans up afterwards.

There is tremendous symbolism connected to food. That you eat this and don't eat that means something. Certain kinds of people eat certain kinds of food. Through our choices and behavior at table, we name and identify ourselves. For example, a vegetarian diet has been a conscious choice for some because they've studied the politics of food: who eats meat and who can't eat meat; what eating meat is doing not only to our health but even to the planet.

Other scholars continue the theme: "Food exchanges are able to act as symbols of human interaction. Eating is a behavior which symbolizes feelings and relationships, mediates social status and power, expresses the boundaries of group identity" (Gillian Feeley-Harnick, *The Lord's Table: Eucharist and Passover in Early Christianity* [Philadelphia: University of Pennsylvania Press, 1981]).

Whom you eat with defines whom you *don't* eat with. During the years I was pastor of New Jerusalem Community in Cincinnati that was really hard for me. There was one of me and as many as three hundred New Jerusalem community members. It was more symbolic than I ever wanted it to be when I would accept an invitation to somebody's house for supper. If I went to one family's house, I worried that others would be jealous. Eventually I found myself avoiding those invitations, and limiting myself to communal or social obligations.

Another example of food's symbolism is our supermarkets. It's a rare supermarket in the white suburbs that sells chitlins. Most American with European backgrounds don't even know what chitlins are. (They're fried pork rinds, chitterlings.) If you went to a grocery store in a white suburb and asked for chitlins, you would immediately be categorized as a certain type of a person. The same, of course, would be true of a person seeking sushi in a working-class grocery store. Everyone would know that person came from another part of town or was trying to make some kind of statement.

Again, Crossan says:

> Table fellowship or commensalism is not the same as almsgiving; almsgiving is not table fellowship. Generous almsgiving may even be conscience's last great refuge against the terror of open table fellowship!

Jesus never appears to be pushing as such what we call social programs. He is much more radical. He is calling us to a new social order where we literally share table differently! Dorothy Day was apparently right on target when she founded "houses of hospitality" as her primary message of evangelization. The poor are welcomed to the table. Remember Jesus' instructions to the missionaries: The disciples are to go out with no money or traveling bag, or footwear (see Matthew 10:10). They are to be in need of hospitality and enter

79

into other people's worlds and mercy.

My father Saint Francis of Assisi took this very literally. That kept the early Franciscans on the move so we couldn't become an establishment and force the people to come to us. Francis went out into the world of the poor, entering into it on their terms. Can you imagine if we had taken Jesus' commands to the missionaries seriously, how different the evangelization of Mexico would have been? What if we had not brought along all of our European baggage to the evangelization of the New World?

Indeed, those Gospel instructions are the only directives Jesus gave us. He didn't tell missionaries to teach the Creed or the Trinity. He simply said don't take any traveling bag, don't take any money in your belt. That's why Francis wore a rope. A belt was a wallet and he wanted to show he didn't have any money. He was totally dependent upon the poor to enter into their world. What extraordinary symbolism! Both Jesus and Francis entered into others' worlds and let them invite the disciples as their house guests. In that way grace, life, could be poured back and forth. How beautiful! It has the ring of truth. Many missionaries are rediscovering it today.

Consider your own relationships with those who invite you over to eat at their home. Sharing table fellowship repeatedly builds a history of trust. To build that trust is as simple as entering into their house and accepting hospitality. That kind of trust has taken me through some hard times with friends—times when others turned against me. The people with whom I ate were willing to stand beside me even when they didn't understand what I was going through. We had sat side-by-side as equals around a table. I had come into their world, without society's pretenses, as their friend and confidante. Eating together in one another's homes changes the nature of social relationship radically, much more than we might have thought.

The mystery of sharing food and a common table takes place on different levels. First there is the unifying idea of sharing the same food. Then there is the whole symbolism of the table itself: where you sit at the table, how the table is arranged. Together, the food and table become a symbol of how your social world is arranged. Once you rearrange life around the table you begin to change your notions of social life.

That, I believe, was Jesus' most consistent social action: eating in new ways! In the midst of that eating, he announced the Kingdom and talked in new ways. Usually on his way in or out of the house he encountered those who were oppressed and eliminated from the system. A great number of Jesus' healings and exorcisms take place while he's either entering a house to have a meal with someone or leaving a house after just having had a meal with someone. He redefines where power is on many different levels at the same time. Religious power is, for one thing, mostly exercised *outside* the Temple and synagogue.

It is necessary to calculate very carefully what was lost and what was gained as Christianity developed. The Church moved from Jesus' real meal with open table fellowship to its continuance in the relatively safe ritual meal that became the Christian Eucharist. Unfortunately, the meal itself came to redefine social reality in a negative way, in terms of worthiness and unworthiness. That is almost exactly the opposite of Jesus' intention! To this day we use Eucharist to define membership in terms of worthy and unworthy. Even if we deny that is our intention, it is clearly the practical message that people hear. We must ask whether people work out relationships independently and then come over for supper (sometimes), or if the invitation to come over for supper is not the healing way to work out the relationship.

Second, it is strange and inconsistent that sins of marriage and sexuality seem to be the only ones that exclude from the table, even when other sins like greed and hatefulness are more of a public scandal.

What is Jesus accused of by his contemporaries? By one side, of eating with tax collectors and sinners (Matthew 9:10-11, for example); and by the other side, of eating too much (Luke 7:34), or with the Pharisees and lawyers (Luke 7:36-50, 11:37-54, 14:1). He ate with both sides. He ate with lepers (Mark 14:3), he received a woman with a bad name at a men's dinner (Luke 7:36-37) and even invited himself over to a "sinner's" house (Luke 19:1-10). He didn't please anybody, it seems—always breaking the rules and spreading out the table.

A Universal Table

But don't take just the scholars' word for it. Let's examine the New Testament itself. The most powerful examples are in Mark and Luke. Why not Matthew? Because Matthew's Gospel is addressed to a first-century equivalent of the middle class. Matthew, for example, takes "How blessed are you who are poor" (Luke 6:20b) and softens it a bit into "How blessed are the poor in spirit" (Matthew 5:3a). He's trying to prevent his "middle class" audience from writing him off at the outset. The open table fellowship is very often weakened in Matthew's Gospel compared to Mark and Luke. Mark and Luke are the harder, more challenging Gospels.

In light of that softness, Matthew's Gospel is probably well suited for most of us. Middle-class people can hear Matthew more quickly than they can hear Luke. Luke is talking to the poor in a way that will make them feel invited and accepted by God. Mark is doing the same thing for people with a little more security, it seems. This is a good example of how we should speak in a way that enables us to be heard. (Paul is a master at this, and proud of it; see 1 Corinthians 9:19-23.)

Luke 14 is one of the most powerful passages. In the first sentence of that chapter there are two shocking things which we probably miss on Sunday because they come at the very beginning of the reading. (We're barely settled into our seats and the first sentence is over already!) "Now it happened that on a Sabbath day he had gone to share a meal in the house of one of the leading Pharisees..." (14:1a). That sets the stage: Jesus entering totally into the world of the establishment on a highly regulated day, a day when all good Jews should do certain things and should not do other things.

Jesus is in place to break all kinds of rules and to upset lots of people. He's eating with the cultural and religious establishment, the leading Pharisees. That in itself is undoubtedly upsetting the social activists in town, the liberals. Can't you hear them: "What is he doing going over and eating in Northeast Heights with the rich people!"

"...[A]nd they watched him closely" (14:1b). These are the passive-aggressive types. They appear to be his friends, but they're just waiting for him to slip up. It's very hard to win in such situations, as you know. They want to see what this man is really about. We'll invite him to our house, and see what he's up to. "Now there in front of him was a man with dropsy"—how this man got in we're not told—"and Jesus addressed the lawyers and Pharisees with the words, 'Is it against the law to cure someone on the Sabbath, or not?' But they remained silent..." (14:2-4a). The pernicious nature of passive-aggressive people is that they maintain a positive self-image while on another level wishing or intending ill.

It's also one of those cases where they knew no matter what they answered they'd displease someone, so they kept their mouths shut. "[S]o he took the man and cured him and sent him away. Then he said to them"—he knows they're upset, he knows they're trying to get him, so he challenges them—" 'Which of you here, if his son falls into a well, or his ox, will not pull him out on a Sabbath day without any hesitation?' And to this they could find no answer" (14:5b-6).

This first example is fundamental. The law at this period of Jewish history is being interpreted almost exclusively through the Book of Leviticus, particularly 17—24, the Law of Holiness. That interpretation is characterized by: (1) obeying the law literally, (2) ritual observance of cult and (3) keeping one's group and group symbols pure. Holiness is thought of as a separatist purity. Such an emphasis continually reemerges in right-wing movements in every age: correct code, cult and community.

Exclusion and inclusion issues are absolutely central to the Law of Holiness. And this is what Jesus takes on front and center, his own tradition from the Torah. He refuses to interpret the Mosaic law in terms of Leviticus's Law of Holiness, in terms of inclusion/exclusion, the symbolic self-identification of Judaism as the righteous, pure, elite group.

Jesus continually interprets the Law of Holiness in terms of the God whom he has met—and that God is always *compassion* and *mercy*. Harvard psychologist Lawrence Kohlberg describes six stages in human moral development from infancy. Jesus is the person at Lawrence Kohlberg's sixth level of morality (enlightenment), largely preaching to people at levels two and three (selfish need and peer pressure), and an institution that doesn't want people who go beyond level four and a half (socially defined roles for the common good), because then you won't idolize the institution anymore.

When the law gets in the way of human compassion Jesus simply disregards the law. He has found its *meaning*. As he says most clearly about picking and eating grain on the sabbath (see Mark 2:23-28), the law is not an end in itself. It's a means to an end. The Law was made for humanity; humanity was not made for the Law, Jesus says (see Mark 2:27).

That's cataclysmic. It undercuts most of institutional religion since the beginning of time. Religion tends to idolize law, to make group boundaries and the symbols of the group ends in themselves. At that point Jesus departs from what would become rabbinic Judaism and sets out on a path that eventually would become Christianity. (Although the same pattern will be repeated there, as it always is in every life.)

Surely that is not the way he thought about it, though. When dying on the cross, in his human mind he must have fully thought of himself as a good Jewish man, not the founder of Christianity (much less the Roman Catholic Church, Methodist Church or any other Church!). We don't want to hear that. But that's who Jesus was: a good Jew who is trying to reform Judaism in terms of moving out the boundaries. As one who has tasted God's infinite love, he has a vision that defies society's boundaries. He moves them out so much that Paul then goes out and invites the Gentiles in. Peter (and those closest to him) wasn't ready for that, as we see in Acts 11:15 and Galatians 2. Yet Jesus created the possibility of a universal religion for all nations. He was not the kind of Messiah that Judaism expected or even wanted.

The reason Christianity has the power to be a universal religion is precisely because of this doctrine of open table fellowship (which the other monotheistic religions do not teach so clearly, except at the mystical level. For us, it should be first-level teaching.). If only people who rightly accept Jesus as their "exclusive savior" would also accept his teaching of utter *inclusivity!* Too often we seem to worship the messenger almost as an avoidance of the message. The ego will use any subterfuge to remain in control.

Now let's get back to Jesus' dinner conversation with the leading Pharisees in Luke 14.

> He then told the guests a parable, because he had noticed how they picked the places of honor. He said this, "When someone invites you to a wedding feast, do not take your seat in the place of honour. A more distinguished person than you may have been invited, and the person who invited you both may come and say, 'Give up your place to this man.' And then, to your embarrassment, you will have to go and take the lowest place. No; when you are a guest, *make your way to the lowest place and sit there*, so that, when your host comes, he may say, 'My friend, move up higher.' Then, everyone with you at the table will see you honoured...."
>
> Then he said to his host, "When you give a lunch or a dinner, do not invite your friends or your brothers or your relations or rich neighbours, in case they invite you back and so repay you. No; when you have a party, invite the poor, the crippled, the lame, the blind; *then you will be blessed, for they have no means to repay you* and so you will be repaid when the upright rise again."
>
> On hearing this, one of those gathered round the table said to him, "Blessed is anyone who will share the meal in the kingdom of God!" (Luke 14:7-10, 12-15, emphases added.)

The Kingdom table is one where, first of all, insiders are not seeking status. It's a table that does not honor class, but in fact prefers what Matthew finally calls the least of the brothers and sisters: the crippled, the lame and the blind, the little outsiders. In his description of banquet tables, Jesus undercuts all meritocracy and proclaims "blessed" those who opt out of the game or those excluded from society.

What follows in Luke 14:15-24 is a third banquet parable, the one where the invited guests all offer excuses for not coming to a wedding feast. Notice that these are *good* excuses; these are not bad people. One had bought a piece of land, another had bought five oxen that required his attention, the third is a newlywed. These are nice proper folks doing appropriate things. (The call to the gospel

85

life is not really a call to be moral, law-abiding and "good," although many seem to think so. It is, rather, *to follow Jesus*—who keeps us on the path of letting go and rediscovering, which is very different from just "being good." Think about that!)

Historians claim that the law may never have been more carefully observed than during this period of Jewish history. The Jews of Jesus' day, including those who played a part in Jesus' death, were *not* bad people! If I wanted to say what killed Jesus, it was not bad people; it was *good people following conventional wisdom*. Unless you understand that, the essential conflict of the Gospels will never hit you. Those who rejected Jesus were doing all the right things. They were nice Jewish citizens who had not yet heard about the Reign of God.

If you forget the rest of this book, please remember just this: Religion is all the things you normally go through to meet God. The gospel is the way you will see and think *after* you have met God! The gospel is the effect of the God-encounter; religion, though it often stirs desire, is also the most common and disguised way of *avoiding* the encounter! The parable ends on an ominous note: "...[N]ot one of those who were invited shall have a taste of my banquet" (Luke 14:24). Religion is the invite; the gospel is the banquet.

Eating With Sinners

Jesus' "Code of Compassion" is found in Mark (2:13-15) as well:

> He went out again to the shore of the lake; and all the people came to him, and he taught them. As he was walking along he saw Levi the son of Alphaeus sitting at the tax office, and he said to him, "Follow me." And he got up and followed him.
> When Jesus was at dinner in his house, a number of tax collectors and sinners were also sitting at table with Jesus and his disciples; *for there were many of them among his followers* (emphasis added).

Apparently, this Levi is a tax collector, one of the people who were ripping off the poor and pocketing plenty of money. Jesus calls Levi from this group who are the oppressors, and goes immediately to eat at his house. By going there he is already moving his disciples beyond their comfort zone. It is easy to imagine Simon the Zealot and Judas remaining outside, grumbling.

The word *sinners* usually conjures up for us notions of judgment and morality. In Jesus' day, sinners were clearly defined by the Levitical Law of Holiness. That definition is not the same as today, at least on the surface. In those days, you were either a sinner or not a sinner, and everybody knew which one you were. If you were not able to follow the purification rules, the debt codes and the purity codes, you knew you were a sinner, and others did too. It was an objective category more than a subjective accusation.

These codes, ironically, created more and more sinners. In Jesus' day there was an increasing emphasis on the codes. You had to jump the hoops at the Temple and pay money to jump each hoop. Thus, it was getting so that lots of people couldn't afford *not* to be sinners, because their location, job or money kept them from ritual observance. Shepherds were in this category, for example, which might enlighten your reading of the Christmas story.

How horrible those times were, you might say. Yet in today's society we do much the same thing. We wouldn't openly give such a moral tinge to poverty, but our society still looks down on the people who can't pay their way. Consider the shameful way people talk about welfare recipients. In the Gospels, wherever you read "sinners" it simply refers to the people who can't do it right—very often because they can't afford the Temple fees. It might drive the point home for modern Americans to read these passages replacing "sinners" with "people on welfare" or unemployed, uneducated, homeless, in jail—the effect is the same.

Back to our story:

> When the scribes of the Pharisee party saw him eating with sinners and tax collectors, they said to his disciples, "Why does he eat with tax collectors and sinners?" (Mark 2:16).

Just when his good disciples were about to say, "I wish I knew!" Jesus said to them,

> It is not the healthy who need the doctor, but the sick. I
> came to call not the upright, but sinners (Mark 2:17b-c).

Jesus does not see his task as gathering an elite of the "saved," but founding a general hospital for the throwaways.

It is easy for us to write off these scribes and Pharisees as self-righteous, arrogant people. But it isn't that. They feel bound by the shame and honor codes that shape their lives. They're just doing what's expected. But Jesus isn't, so he challenges them. By eating with tax collectors and sinners—and accepting no shame—Jesus is discounting the only world they know. We would react the same way, I'm sure, with outrage and scandal!

This tension comes up anywhere Jesus confronts the rules that allowed the religious elite to feel more righteous than anyone else. In fasting, for example, Jesus observes that the elite would have a problem with him no matter what he did: They wouldn't listen to John, who wouldn't eat or drink, and now Jesus comes along eating and drinking and they don't like him either (see Matthew 11:18-19). It's obvious to Jesus they just don't want the truth. He says he would rather sin on the side of eating and drinking, which probably upsets them more. (I wonder what vegetarians and Baptists do with that text?)

Now let's look at this call of Matthew in Matthew's Gospel:

> As Jesus was walking on from there he saw a man named
> Matthew [who apparently is the same as Levi] sitting at the
> tax office, and he said to him, "Follow me." And he got up
> and followed him (9:9).

The quick response of several of the disciples seems to name the quality Jesus is looking for: risk-takers over security freaks. Anybody who has worked with personnel knows the difference.

The story continues, just as in Mark, but with a different interpretation.

> Now while he was at table in the house it happened that a
> number of tax collectors and sinners came to sit at the table
> with Jesus and his disciples. When the Pharisees saw this,
> they said to his disciples, "Why does your master eat with
> tax collectors and sinners?" (9:10-11)

And Jesus repeats his line the same as in Mark: "It is not the healthy who need the doctor, but the sick" (9:12). It seems to me that Jesus is saying *relationship* reality is above *ritual* reality. People are more important than ideology. Thus we are to go where we're needed. We are to go where we're invited. We are to go where life is wanted and where it is received. "Go and learn the meaning of the words: Mercy is what pleases me, not sacrifice" (Matthew 9:13).

Undoubtedly Jesus says this because in the desert he met a God of mercy and remembered this not-so-quoted line from Hosea:

> [F]or faithful love is what pleases me, not sacrifice;
> knowledge of God, not burnt offerings (Hosea 6:6).

This is the God that Jesus called Father, Abba. It's not that Jesus is a liberal or one who thinks boundaries don't matter. No, he has met the God who is "mercy, within mercy, within mercy" (in Thomas Merton's words).

Meeting that kind of God allows you to proclaim a gospel of mercy, above and beyond the formulations of those who quote but do not know. The authority of Jesus—unlike the good scribes—is that he *knows* for himself, and calls us to know for ourselves.

When I see political correctness on the left becoming just as rigid and righteous as patriotic correctness on the right, I know again that Jesus was very wise. The Church, as Jesus seems to be defining it, is the gathering of accepted brokenness. It's *not* the gathering of the saved. (Matthew 9:13 is the final punch line: "And indeed I came to call not the upright, but sinners.")

The Church is never a "members-only" club. Isn't it sad that the Church became the gathering of the saved instead of what Jesus makes it in his open table of fellowship? Jesus' table is the gathering of the *un*saved! Sometimes fellow priests tell me, "We're preaching to the choir. We're saving the saved. We just keep gathering the same two hundred people, sing Jesus songs and read the Bible. And we convince one another that we're saved and that we're holy." That's what happens when the Church becomes established in one place, when the people come to the Church instead of us going to them. We create the congregation of the "enlightened"—who by that very token are not enlightened at all.

The message is clear: What we normally call morality is simply not what Jesus was into. Jesus redefines reality in terms of who-God-is—not little people's moral categories about what makes me good and you bad. The God-encounter, of course, demands a much higher morality of us than creed, code or cult ever would.

We see that Jesus gets very impatient with external religion when he goes to the house of a Pharisee. As I mentioned before, Jesus eats with the elite, but he always challenges them. He seems to have forgotten Miss Manners' rules for guests:

> ...[A] Pharisee invited him to dine at his house. He went in and sat down at table. The Pharisee saw this and was surprised that he had not first washed before the meal. But the Lord said to him, "You Pharisees! You clean the outside of cup and plate, while inside yourselves you are filled with extortion and wickedness. Fools! Did not he who made the outside make the inside too?" (Luke 11:37b-40).

The point of the passage is this: Worry about the inner attitude instead of being preoccupied with the outer ritual:

> "[Y]ou pay your tithe of mint and rue and all sorts of garden herbs and neglect justice and the love of God! These you should have practiced, without neglecting the others" (11:42b).

It's never either/or for Jesus; it's a matter of sequence, priority and motivation: Get the center point clear and then the rituals are OK. Rituals are not to be idolized; they are only rituals.

But Jesus never throws them out, either (liberals, take heed!). People need to have a symbolic and celebrated universe. There is no healthy religion without metaphor, symbol or ritual. Without some creed, code and cult a group will make no impact on the world or themselves as a community. The temptation today is to revert to private enlightenment with no accountability systems or community base.

In the rest of Luke 11 Jesus uses table fellowship to challenge the entire religious system. You'll see that his greatest challenges come with those who are thinking well of themselves. There is another strong example in Luke 7:36-50, Simon the Pharisee:

> One of the Pharisees invited him to a meal. When he
> arrived at the Pharisee's house and took his place at table,
> suddenly a woman came in... (7:36-37a).

Now, it's men only at meals. Just like the Greek "symposium"
where great ideas and food were shared. That's the only world they
know. Woman's place is in the kitchen (which is the whole
meaning of the Martha/Mary story in Luke 10—Martha becomes
upset when Mary leaves the kitchen. Women are in the outer rooms,
just as they are in the outer courts of the Temple.).

In this story, not only does this woman crash a male symposium
and dinner party—like a woman crashing the Eagles' Club
meeting—but this woman had a bad name in town. She had heard
he was dining with the Pharisee and had brought with her an
alabaster jar of ointment. You know the story: "She waited behind
him at his feet...." (That's *behind* Jesus because at a meal the men
all reclined on the floor, heads closest to the center, where you can
have food and good conversation for hours on end.)

> She waited behind him at his feet, weeping, and her tears
> fell on his feet, and she wiped them away with her hair;
> then she covered his feet with kisses and anointed them
> with the ointment. (Luke 7:38)

Anyone knows what a group of men would assume when they saw
that. Imagine the snickering! Uncovered hair was surely not a
symbol of an upright or attached woman. And she kisses him—and
he lets her. What must this imply! What happened between Jesus
and this woman?

> When the Pharisee who had invited him saw this, he said to
> himself, "If this man were a prophet, he would know who
> this woman is and what sort of person it is who is touching
> him and what a bad name she has." Then Jesus took him up
> and said, "Simon, I have something to say to you." (Luke
> 7:39-40a)

Jesus never shames people. He just says the truth, which probably
shames people sometimes, but that's not his intention.

He replied, "Say on, Master." "There was once a creditor
who had two men in his debt; one owed him five hundred
denarii, the other fifty. They were unable to pay, so he let
them both off. Which of them will love him more?" Simon
answered, "The one who was let off more, I suppose."
Jesus said, "You are right." (Luke 7:40b-43)

Then he turned to the woman and said to Simon, "You
see this woman? I came into your house, and you poured
no water over my feet, but she has poured out her tears
over my feet and wiped them away with her hair. You gave
me no kiss, but she has been covering my feet with kisses
ever since I came in. You did not anoint my head with oil,
but she has anointed my feet with ointment. For this reason
I tell you that *her sins, many as they are, have been
forgiven her, because she has shown such great love.*"
(Luke 7:39-47a, emphasis added)

That's a very interesting turn of phrase. We would probably say a
loving person will forgive, but Jesus says a forgiven person will
know how to love. Sin itself, the anguish of alienation, the joy of
reunion are all parts of the economy of salvation for Jesus:

"It is someone who is forgiven little who shows little
love." Then he said to her, "Your sins are forgiven." Those
who were with him at table began to say to themselves,
"Who is this man, that even forgives sins?' " (Luke
7:47b-49).

Their worldview of meritocracy and cultic forgiveness has just
been ignored. Somebody just lost their commission down at the
Temple.

Jesus is transferring what was normally done in the Temple to
the home. He is announcing the forgiveness of sins freely. And this
was normally tied up in a highly ritualized kind of religion at the
Temple. "But he said to the woman, 'Your faith has saved you; go
in peace' " (Luke 7:50). With that, Jesus redefines the boundaries—
and availability—of holiness.

A Second Kind of Meal

The tradition of table fellowship shows up elsewhere in the

New Testament; for example, the several loaves and fishes accounts in the Gospels (Matthew 14:13-21; 15:32-39; Mark 6:30-44; 8:1-10; Luke 9:10-17; John 6:1-13). Scholars say now that even while Jesus was still alive, there seemed to be two traditions of open table fellowship: one of bread and wine, the other of bread and fish. The bread and wine finally won out—that meal is what we call the Mass today.

But the bread and fishes stories point to an open table fellowship tradition, too. The exciting thing about these stories is that they emphasize surplus and outside guests. At the end of each of them, there are seven or twelve baskets left over. That surplus seems to be a point of this form of table fellowship. It's a type of meal we'd call a potluck supper today. Apparently Jesus invited everybody together to bring their food and there was plenty for all the poor and then some.

It's unfortunate that we lost the bread and fishes ritual meal. Because the bread and wine ritual meal didn't emphasize this idea of surplus, real food that actually fed the poor. The bread and wine tradition lent itself more to cult and ritualization. The bread and fish tradition, if retained, might have contributed to issues of justice, community and social reordering.

We see this after the Resurrection for example. In John 21:1-14 the apostles are out on the lake. They see Jesus on the shore, cooking fish at a charcoal fire. He invites them to come share bread and the fishes.

If you remember what happened after Jesus' arrest, you see the significance of this charcoal fire. The only other charcoal fire in the Gospels is the one Peter stood at when he betrayed Jesus (see John 18:18). Jesus invites him now to another charcoal fire, where they share the bread and the fishes. And he says, in effect, "Peter, it's OK. Forget it." At this second charcoal fire the risen Jesus initiates table fellowship with Peter, who just a few days before rejected, betrayed and abandoned him in his hour of need. It seems the bread and fish meal also had a healing, reconciling significance. What a shame we have lost this.

That passage opens the way for us to appreciate the familiar conflict in Saint Paul's First Letter to Corinthians. Written in the 50's, it shows how long the tradition of open table fellowship must have hung on.

> ...[I]t is not the Lord's Supper that you eat; for when the
> eating begins, each one of you has his own supper first,
> and there is one going hungry while another is getting
> drunk. Surely you have homes for doing your eating and
> drinking in? Or have you such disregard for God's
> assembly that you can put to shame those who have
> nothing? What am I to say to you? Congratulate you? On
> this I cannot congratulate you. (11:20-22)

Later eucharistic theologians don't know what to do with this text.
Clearly the first-century Church had a very different understanding
of Eucharist than we do now. Clearly it was a sharing of real food,
not a priest standing at an altar with bread and wine. You get that
from the text. The explanation was that these were agape meals
(ancient potlucks), not the real Eucharist. But very likely the
eucharistic celebration was joined to a meal. *It was* the potluck
supper in which we all came together. The rich people could bring
rich food, the poor people would bring chitlins. Paul could be
saying that it's not the Lord's Supper because the proper social
arrangement is not there. If he's saying Jesus would not come into
such a meal, this is revolutionary theology by later Church criteria.

We really have no eyewitness accounts of the Last Supper. We
have the Gospel accounts, but none of the twelve apostles who were
at the Last Supper wrote the Gospels. The Gospels were written
from the 70's to the 90's. Certainly there was a good oral tradition.
But it is very likely that the Last Supper was a Passover meal of
open table fellowship—the final one of many among Jesus and his
closest followers—that evolved into a ritualized offering of bread
and wine. The disciples had come to understand it as a way of
gathering, as the way to define their reality and their relationship to
one another. It became for them a powerful symbol of unity, of
giving and sharing, of breaking the self and giving the self over.

Yet the ritual became very succinct, as we see in our earliest
record of the Eucharist:

> "For the tradition I received from the Lord and also handed
> on to you is that on the night he was betrayed, the Lord
> Jesus took some bread, and after he had given thanks, he

broke it, and he said, 'This is my body, which is for you; do this in remembrance of me' " (1 Corinthians 11:23-24).

Now we get to the heart of Saint Paul's argument for maintaining the new social order at Eucharist:

> Everyone is to examine himself and only then eat of the bread or drink from the cup; because a person who eats and drinks *without recognizing the body* is eating and drinking his own condemnation (1 Corinthians 11:28-29, emphasis added).

Very possibly, the two traditions are coming together here: bread and wine plus potluck agape meal. Unfortunately the second was lost, perhaps because of the very difficulties of class it was trying to address. Yes, we are to recognize Jesus himself in the Eucharist, but we are also to recognize the living Body of Christ too. For the first thousand years the Latin term *corpus verum*, the "true body," referred to the assembly. The people were the true Body of Christ in the assembly. When the true Body said through the mouth of the presider, "This is my body," the bread and the wine became the symbol of the living Body. The bread and wine were the *corpus mysticum*. These usages were completely reversed in time.

There is no Eucharist without an assembly. During the centuries of private Masses we held onto that tradition (barely!) by requiring an altar boy. But clearly the Eucharist was meant to be a sacrificial meal in which the Body recognized itself, defined itself, declared its social identity and its central purpose, which was to be Jesus in space and time, to live in a new world order of true sisterhood and brotherhood (meal), of redemptive suffering and solidarity (sacrifice).

I want to close this chapter—and Part I of this book—on a contemporary note. We need to consider and reconsider the symbolism of food in our own lives. In retreat houses and homes across the land, people are starting to reevaluate the social, political, economic and nutritional meaning of food. America's love affair with beef for example, and the disastrous effects that is having on the Third World, has come under question in recent years. Rain forests are being cut down, land and resources are being spent so that we can have burgers aplenty.

I was staying with a cattle rancher in California recently, and to his credit he was reading a book describing the ill effects of cattle and beef production on the earth. The first day he wasn't too happy with it. He came in the second night, troubled. (This is a very good Irish Catholic man; there is no doubt in my mind faith is first to him.) He said to me, "Richard, I have to change my life." He saw that his livelihood could well be contributing to starvation overseas. Now that's reconnecting the two meals: because of bread and wine we must do "bread and fish" differently.

That's one contemporary way to consider this gospel message. Food is still a way of being in solidarity with people. What you eat and what you don't eat can be a way of saying, "I want to be in solidarity with certain people who can't have meat three times a day." Meat is the food of the rich. It's the over-proteinization of people in a growing world of already five billion people.

Another example: writer and poet Kathy Coffey wrote a 1995 article in *St. Anthony Messenger* magazine, "A Mother's Perspective on the Eucharist." In it she compares the many acts of a woman, a loving mother and teacher, to the traditional words of institution at Eucharist. "In parenthood," she writes, " 'This is my body' becomes a constant refrain as time flows into launching healthy children: the buttoning, unbuttoning, listening, combing, bathing, encouraging, chauffeuring, story-reading and tucking-in processes of the day.... Into every child I parent, every student I teach and every poem I write, I pour something of myself."

Of "This is my blood," she writes, in part: "When women gather to drink wine, the occasion is often festive. As the burgundy sparkles in the glasses, the laughter bubbles. Sometimes, then, we segue into the heartbreaks revealed only to the closest friends: the lost loves, the tragic betrayals, the spouses and children who disappoint.... From the shared sorrow emerges a new strength."

After ten thousand eatings we begin to believe that we are *what* we eat, we are *who* we eat with, we are *where* we eat, we are *how* we eat, and for believers, we are even *who* we eat: We have "recognized the Body."

Part Two

UNDERSTANDING THE SERMON

Where Jesus Is Heading

To clarify where Jesus is leading us, let me begin the second section with what I hope is a demystifying explanation:

1) **The old self on the old path:** Non-conversion or non-enlightenment.

2) **The old self on a new path:** Where most religion begins and ends: new behavior, new language and practices that are sincere, but the underlying myth/worldview/motivation and goals is never really changed. My anger, fear and ego are merely transferred to now defend *my* idea of God or religion.

3) **The new self on a new path:** The total transformation of consciousness, worldview, motivation, rewards and goals that characterizes *one who loves* and *is loved* by God. This is conversion according to Jesus.

CHAPTER SIX

Joining Heaven and Earth

L et's begin where the Gospels begin. In all four accounts, prominence is given to the character called John the Baptist. He is probably far more important than we have realized. John is Jesus' starting point too. That's what is symbolized by Jesus going to be baptized by John.

The beginning of Matthew 3 says that John the Baptist appeared and preached in the wilderness. This was his message: "Repent [which means 'turn around'], for the kingdom of Heaven is close at hand" (3:2a). In Matthew's very next chapter we will see that exact phrase become Jesus' first line: "Repent, for the kingdom of Heaven is close at hand" (4:17b). Matthew's Jesus is obviously building on John, saying the same thing but going further. It begins, much like religion, in duty or threat. In Jesus it becomes invitation.

John "cries out" in the wilderness (see Matthew 3:3). That's wonderful symbolism, of course. Have you ever heard someone say to a child, maybe in a moment of desperation, "Talking to you is like talking to the wall! I might as well shout to the wind!" That's the telling symbolism of going out and yelling in the wilderness. What John's got to say no one in the establishment system wants to hear or is willing to hear. He's radically questioning the very legitimacy of the existing religious order by doing religious practices on his own authority. John is the symbol of religion's need for constant reform, and the unhearable nature of the message.

The establishment is always sending people out to question John. He is a voice crying in the wilderness, apparently with some success. He refuses to wear the clothes of polite society, but camel hair with a leather belt around his waist. He does not eat the food of society. His food is locusts and wild honey. Notice something sweet and something bitter in John's scant but symbolically rich diet (see also Ezekiel 2:8—3:3). That is always the character of the wisdom figure, one who learns how to eat both. Wisdom puts together the yin and the yang, the dark and the light. John has to eat both the sweetness of life and the tragedy of life.

Matthew's Gospel says, "Then Jerusalem and all Judea and the whole Jordan district made their way to [John]" (Matthew 3:5a). What we saw in Part I explains why he would be a threat. These pilgrims are supposed to be making their way to Jerusalem and instead they're making their way out to hear this upstart in the desert! Among all those comes Jesus himself: "[H]e came from Galilee...to be baptized by John" (3:13b).

In effect, Jesus is legitimating what John is doing, saying it's OK to pour water over people and tell them their sins are forgiven. That's revolutionary. Jews were supposed to follow the Law of Holiness of Leviticus, and suddenly John is making it far too easy to get God to love you, to get God to forgive you. God becomes as available as Jordan River water. And, of course, the irony is that the water is in the desert where water isn't supposed to be. You can find God everywhere, in other words—outside of institutions, official priesthood or formal observance. One wonders if the Church today even catches John's dangerous corrective.

Of course Matthew the Evangelist had trouble with having Jesus baptized for the forgiveness of sin because Matthew's image is he had no sins to be forgiven. So we have Jesus saying, "Leave it like this...; it is fitting that we should, in this way, do all that uprightness demands" (3:15). Jesus doesn't have any trouble with this unofficial rite. He says, in effect, "I want to be a part of the whole human journey. I also agree with John's approach."

As soon as Jesus is baptized, there is a dramatic, mythologized statement of the eternal truth that is happening: He "came up from the water, and suddenly the heavens opened" (3:16b). What does it mean to have the heavens opening? It means two worlds becoming one, the sacred and the secular coming together: the joining of earth and heaven.

I've read the Book of Genesis from the time I was a child, but I marvel that there is always something new to learn. I was surprised to make a wonderful discovery one day: At the end of six days of creation it says, "[A]nd indeed it was very good" (1:31b). Only on one day does God *not* say the work was good: the second day, when heaven is separated from earth. This is the symbolic day when union was ripped apart, separating the sacred and secular, separating the holiness of God and the holiness of the earth.

The work of religion is to put together darkness and light, earth and heaven, and find they're one mystery. Christians' word for that is the Paschal Mystery, whereby we rejoin the separated worlds. Here we have Jesus, the great reconciler, coming to hold them all together. He walks the human path in all of its demands, even submitting to this rite that John the Baptist has created.

That most basic and universal element, water, may be a natural religious symbol. I remember being in Varanasi (formerly Benares), the holy city of pilgrimage on the Ganges River in Uttar Pradesh State in northern India. In the early morning there was dust as far as you could see. I remember the Hindus walking in hordes to the sacred river. There they would strip naked and wash. Hindus believe that washing in the Ganges cleanses them of sin. Washing in water is a universal experience, and a powerful symbol for all renewal. Somehow the spirit needs rituals to symbolize what's happening inside, to use the physical realm as well as ideas to experience metaphor. You cannot break through to the spiritual except through metaphor. You have to enact it, taste it, feel it.

Someone once said all great truths must be veiled: To look at truth directly blinds you. That's why religion has much more to do with poetry, song and imagery than with academics. Take, for example, the Celts before we made Catholics out of them. The religion of Ireland was largely memorization of poetry, nature religion and fertility rites. In poetry, the metaphorical word has the power to break you through to comprehension of the symbol. The very word *symbol* means a "throwing together." In a Japanese haiku poem, for example, for a moment you see the eternal and you see the real, through the very precise and concise use of words.

Now we return to the symbol in Matthew: "And when Jesus had been baptized he at once came up from the water, and suddenly the heavens opened and he saw the Spirit of God descending like a dove and coming down on him' " (3:16c). Note how the dove comes down and alights from nowhere. Grace cannot be created or manufactured from beneath; it always comes from beyond, from no certain place. Otherwise it isn't grace. Try as we might, we cannot manufacture grace. It will always come from nowhere for certain, like a dove coming out of the sky. You say, Where? How? It usually comes when you're in the midst of your sin or your busyness, so you know you didn't create it. *Grace* literally means "free."

Then comes Jesus' great conversion moment: "And suddenly there was a voice from heaven. 'This is my Son, the Beloved; my favour rests on him'" (Matthew 3:17). After this soul-event, Jesus will move on his path. Nothing will stop him. The time leading up to that moment we know little about. It will be a secret forever. What did Jesus do for thirty years? We don't know. Even the infancy accounts, which are only found in Matthew and Luke, don't really agree with one another. Mark and John didn't even find the infancy stories important enough to include in their Gospels. The point of the Gospels is that at thirty the man called Jesus came to know that he was a beloved Son. He came to know it all the way through, in his head, heart, gut, body, soul and spirit. And at that very point, curiously enough, Jesus is "led by the Spirit out into the desert to be put to the test by the devil" (4:1). Quick contrast, it seems.

It is crucial that Jesus is led by the Spirit. There are two wildernesses, two darknesses in the spiritual journey. One you go into by your own stupidity, by your sin, blindness, ignorance and mistakes. We all do that. But there's another darkness. The holy darkness is the darkness that God leads us into, through and beyond. This is a necessary darkness for the journey. In a certain sense, God's darkness is a much better teacher than light. There comes a time when you have to either go deeper into faith or you will turn back, when you have to live *without knowing* or you lose faith altogether. So we have the Spirit leading Jesus into the wilderness, to face the essential darkness.

Three Temptations

My understanding of the three temptations of Christ has shown up in some of my other writings. Yet some of it is worth touching on here, because Matthew presents the temptations in the text

(4:1-10) leading up to the Sermon on the Mount. The three temptations that Jesus must face are the necessary three temptations that every would-be believer, would-be evangelist, would-be Christian must face.

For me they are summarized in this way: The first is the *need to be effective or relevant*, to turn stones into bread (see 4:3), the need to see the fruits of your own action and to meet people's needs. Jesus has to give up that need.

The second is the *need to be right*: to "stand on the parapet of the Temple" (see 4:5). It's the need to use God, to stand on religion for your own purposes. Jesus even has to give up that assurance of being right, an ego need. It is very symbolic that it is the devil who made him stand on the Temple. It's also the only time when the devil quotes Scripture in the entire Bible. Matthew is showing that you can use religion for diabolical purposes. Religion is both good and subject to misuse. Jesus' response is, in effect, "Don't play games with God" (see 4:7).

The third temptation is the *need for power* or control, symbolized by the devil showing Jesus "all the kingdoms of the world and their splendour" (4:8b). Jesus is aware that power has many forms and many disguises in all of us. The devil names the common price for power: "...[F]all at my feet and do me homage" (4:10). Jesus rejects him with finality. "Then the devil left him..." (4:11). Once you refuse to seek power in any form, there is not much that Satan can do to you.

These three demons are in all of our lives: the need to be effective, the need to be right and the need to be powerful or in control. Until those demons have been faced and exorcised you will very likely not preach the gospel; you will preach your own self. It's only after Jesus exorcises these three demons that he sets out on his public ministry.

> As he was walking by the Lake of Galilee he saw two brothers, Simon, who was called Peter, and his brother Andrew; they were making a cast into the lake with their net, for they were fishermen. And he said to them, "Come after me and I will make you fishers of people." And at once they left their nets and followed him. (Matthew 4:18-20)

Did it happen exactly like that? The point is that Jesus gave people major vision and challenge. He thus always appeals to risk-takers. Somehow this man did fascinate people and with some ease they left and followed him. But I find the next paragraph more confounding.

> Going on from there he saw another pair of brothers, James son of Zebedee and his brother John; they were in their boat with their father Zebedee, mending their nets, and he called them. (4:21)

Observe two things: First, they're with their father. There's the patriarchal family—James's and John's loyalties are clearly to Zebedee. Second, they are working. Those are the two sacred cows of kinship culture: family and occupation. You don't call those into question. Yet Jesus does! "And at once, leaving the boat and their father, they followed him" (4:22).

Family and job are not bad things. But falling into easy patterns can keep us from asking new questions about life. (If we are open to love's demands, though, our family relationships can challenge us to the core.) It's significant that Jesus does not tell his followers to stop drinking and burn their *Playboys*—the hot sins—and *then* come and follow. He says leave your father and your nets and come follow me *now*.

The Limits of Family

Jesus tells his followers to leave their families of origin because the families we grow up in keep most people from asking bigger questions. Conventional family wisdom tells you to be a nice kid in your hometown and to do what nice kids in your hometown do. For this reason, most religious founders tell you to leave your family. Call it a necessary detachment, to break away, to get a bigger worldview instead of just filling Mama's and Daddy's dreams for you.

Does this mean you have to leave geographically? Not necessarily (although sometimes it can help). But eventually you must leave them spiritually, psychologically; you must look at their values critically and form your own, not necessarily opposed to theirs, but not theirs just *because* they are your parents' values. It's a necessary part of growing up.

In male-initiation rites worldwide, the boy is always taken away from his mother. Otherwise he'll spend his whole life trying to please Mama or negatively reacting against her. The Catholic priesthood is filled with such men who became priests to please Mama. (Many other professions are, too, I'm sure.) They don't know who they are because that's not really their agenda. They're still living out of their mother's emotional world or doing something to please Dad so they'll finally get his approval.

I know a psychologist who thought she would be so happy when she got her Ph.D. She spent thousands of dollars and worked for years. A week after her graduation, though, she realized the only reason she did it was to get her dad to admire her. And her father didn't even come to the graduation. Now the degree means nothing to her.

Finding one's soul is always leaving one's comfort zone, letting go and going to a bigger place. You can only ask the questions that your milieu allows you to ask. In many organizations, there are questions you cannot ask. Not that there's a law or formal policy, but if you really start asking certain questions, you might have to leave the company or the profession. Can businessmen be critical of maximizing profit at the expense of workers, communities or the environment? Can a military person question individual wars? Will people ever move beyond their families' emotional permissions? Can a woman choose simplicity or the single life if her parents want classy grandchildren?

Jesus creates the *ecclesia*, literally, "the called-out ones." The Church should be that group of people who have moved to a place of freedom and are willing to ask the big questions of the extended family, not only the questions of the natural family.

Like it or not, Jesus in the Gospels says very little that's highly positive about the small family (see Matthew 10:37-39 or 12:46-50). Jesus broadens our vision. Ironically, the neo-conservative movements today often hide behind the word *family*. Yet "family values" is sometimes a cover for a very self-protective and narrow agenda. This is true in Europe, in Latin America and here in the United States. For some reason, a positive buzzword is usually sufficient to cover up another agenda.

Jesus requires his first disciples to call into question even their families and "family values." In our own time, we've discovered that call in a new way. Many people have recognized that if you don't break from a dysfunctional family, you become a part of the sickness yourself. The Twelve-Step movement has taught us to recognize what is sick about our families and what is good about them. For some, that means separating from the family, then freely entering back into them when there's the possibility of love and forgiveness. Leaving our "father and our nets" may also involve questioning our career choices, our family prejudices and our class perspective.

Reclaiming Our Identity

> He went round the whole of Galilee teaching in their synagogues, proclaiming the good news of the kingdom and curing all kinds of disease and illness among the people. (Matthew 4:23)

Much of the Gospels is about either Jesus' preaching or healing. By our later, rational, scientific thinking we may want to throw out all of the healings and miracles of Jesus. But we can't. They are too central to the Gospels. My assumption is that power came out from Jesus. I believe that because I've seen so many physical healings in my own lifetime, and even in my own body (of a serious case of hypoglycemia at Lourdes in 1981 and of malignant melanoma after being prayed over and having surgery in 1992).

In the New Jerusalem community we had astounding healings that to this day I cannot explain. The most dramatic happened when the community was young. I was praying over a whole group of young people. A young woman with cerebral palsy who had never before walked easily stood up and walked straight toward me. To this day she walks, though with a limp. I *know* there is such a thing as physical healing. Yet the Western scientific mind doesn't believe that anymore. We don't believe that when we pray over people God's power sometimes comes through us and we are instruments for healing. Could it be that we don't believe in the active and contemporary power of Jesus in the world? (see James 5:14-15).

There is a social symbolism always latent in Jesus' body miracles. That is not to say that the miracle didn't really happen. Jesus apparently performed hundreds of healing miracles. The ones chosen for the text always have layers of meaning. For example, a blindness miracle will follow an episode of the disciples' spiritual blindness. Jesus will be talking to his disciples, they won't get the point and he'll heal someone who's deaf. There is the passage in Mark (5:26) where it says the woman with the hemorrhage had lost her whole life's savings to the medical profession. The healing story might well be a judgment on such injustice. In this case, *power goes out from him* (see Mark 5:30) like a laser beam finding its destination.

Jesus' miracles are acts of social protest, of taking back necessary power. He's telling the people, "You've got to own your own identity and purpose. Don't let the medical profession, the priestly or legal profession name you or own you." To this day, we surrender our God-given power to them, rather than understanding the gifts that have already been given us for spiritual health, physical health and organizing our own lives. Jesus' innocuous word for this power is *faith*, and he usually praises people for it after they have moved beyond their victim stance.

The sick in Jesus' time were caught in a circle of double victimization. First of all, remember the tax system (Chapter Four). They had to give at least two-thirds to the ruler and the ruling class and then live on the final third. There were other kinds of tolls and fees imposed even on the final third. People who are either poor or taxed into poverty obviously are not going to be able to afford—even in Jesus' time—good health care. So bodily illness undoubtedly occurred in many people because they were oppressed and could not afford a doctor. Frankly, that is still the case for two-thirds of the world's population.

But then, to add insult to injury, the belief system at that time was that your sin made you sick (see John 9:2; Luke 13:1-5). And as if that weren't enough, there were Temple fees, administered by the scribes, the religious lawyers, that were required to pay for the necessary ritual materials and animals in order to be made clean again. You could really call it *triple* victimization: forced poverty, false guilt and then the financial hardship that came with the rituals.

Let us return to the temptations for a moment. Notice that the first two temptations are preceded by this phrase: "If you are Son of God..." (Matthew 4:3 and 4:6). It was perhaps Jesus' greatest temptation and his greatest act of faith. *If* you are Son of God: That's the existential temptation that you and I face every day, the doubt as to *who we are*, where we came from, whether our names are written in heaven, whether we are children of God.

Jesus claimed and believed the divine image within him, and quite straightforwardly told us to do the same. That may be the whole gospel in one sentence.

Repentance: 'My Kingdom Go'

Jesus prefaces his announcement of the Kingdom with a strange word, *repent*. *Repent* is a throwaway word now. We see cartoons of prophets in sandwich boards saying, "Repent." It has this sort of corny, "churchy" meaning to it: Beat yourself, or, Get religion!

The word is so misused, yet we don't dare throw it out. Just when we in the Church have become ashamed of repentance, psychology and therapy have rediscovered it. If you don't repent—in other words if you don't change—you die. If you don't repent of your past mistakes you repeat them. You repeat them again and again and become a very sick person. The addictive society understands this better than the Church does now. Isn't that strange? The Twelve-Step programs tell you to repent, to stop destructive behavior, but if I as a priest say repent, I'm accused of laying guilt. When you don't recognize what is wrong in your actions and why it is wrong, you are almost sure to do that wrong again, maybe just with a different pretext.

I've told gatherings in Germany that because many Germans have never yet repented the Second World War, they're going to repeat it. It is as certain as the dawn that America will continue to be a militaristic, violent country because we have never repented any of our wars. Grief and repentance are the only appropriate Christian response to *any* war, never a victory parade. At very best, wars are a necessary evil, which we can never celebrate or romanticize. Perhaps we need "wailing walls."

I would like to say that the same ultimate reaction is perhaps true for divorce, abortion and various forms of abuse: the appropriate healing and helpful response is probably some ritual of lamentation, sorrow, grieving, naming, forgiving, letting go and going on. This useless shaming and blaming and holding one another forever accountable for past mistakes all comes about, in my opinion, because secular culture has no way to repent. We are finding that the system, without a gospel of healing repentance, is actually more unforgiving than the Church ever was. All it has is the law, which kills, but Jesus has offered us the Spirit, which gives life (see 2 Corinthians 3:6).

Repentance is not an outdated concept; you must repent. *Metanoia* (*convertere* in Latin) means "to turn around." Jesus helped people to change, but he never tried to bully or shame them into it. I hope that we are going to learn from him in addressing many of our social and personal sins.

Kingdom Misperceptions

The concept of the Kingdom is absolutely central to Jesus. It is his core metaphor. If you don't understand the idea of Kingdom, you don't understand Jesus' teaching, because much of Jesus' teaching is describing the Kingdom. Jesus repeats the words of John the Baptist, "Repent, for the kingdom of Heaven is close at hand" (Matthew 3:2; 4:17b).

The Greek word for *kingdom* in the New Testament is *basileia*. In our culture today, the word *kingdom* has sexist connotations for many. After all, kingdoms are run by kings, who can only be men. An equally valid translation for the word *basileia* (although it doesn't have many historical connotations because we haven't used it as much) is the "reign of God." The important denotation is the issue of control, command, oversight, having "a Lord" as organizing principle. Sometimes I sense that this is what a postmodern world actually resists and resents, even though the only real alternative is that I myself become the organizing principle.

In order to explain this concept of the Kingdom or the Reign of God, it may help first to say what it's not. The Kingdom—and this is the most frequent mistake—is not the same as heaven. The

Kingdom is not where you go after you die, eternal life. Yet Christians of all denominations in the West use the term in this way. The scenario is something like this: You die, you go to Saint Peter, who has the keys to the gates of the Kingdom, and he lets you in. That idea is disproven by Jesus' very prayer: "Thy kingdom come, they will be done *on earth* as it is in heaven." As always, Jesus is still joining earth and heaven.

"Thy kingdom come" means very clearly that the Kingdom is something that enters into this world, or, as Jesus puts it, "is close at hand." Don't project it into another world. It's a reality that breaks into this world now and then, when people are like God. The Kingdom is the Really Real (with two capital *R*s). When the Really Real happens, when the true self emerges, you have a taste of what Jesus says it's all about! When that can happen in terms of structures or groups, when you have a free group of people who love the truth more than themselves, then you have a taste of the Kingdom descending to earth.

God gives us just enough tastes of the Kingdom to believe in it and to want it more than anything. It's always now-and-not-yet. If you take all of the parables of Jesus discussed earlier, he never says the Kingdom is totally now or totally later. We only have the first fruits of the Kingdom in this world, but enough to know that it's the only thing that will ever satisfy us. For once you have had the truth, you can't be satisfied with half-truths any more. The Kingdom is the experience of the love of God, the ultimate and real truth. In its light, everything else is relative, even your own life.

I hope you've met at least one Kingdom person in your life. They are surrendered people. You sense that life is OK at their core. They have given control to Another and are at peace. A Kingdom person lives for what matters, for life in its deepest sense. There's a kind of gentle absolutism about their life-style, a kind of calm freedom. Kingdom people feel like grounded yet spacious people. Whatever they are after, they already seem to be enjoying it—and seeing it in unlikely places. Kingdom people make you want to be like them. Mother Teresa is an obvious and well-known example of this type of person; so is the Brazilian Archbishop Dom Helder Camara or Anglican Archbishop Desmond Tutu of South Africa.

But most Kingdom people lead much more ordinary lives. She

might be a cashier at the grocery store who is joyful even under pressure. Her smile might be the inspiration that means hope for a single mother racing through the checkout line on her way to pick up kids at day-care and face an evening of child care alone. He might be the real estate agent who, through his inner peace, conveys to a new family in town that everything will be all right. Kingdom people are anchored by their awareness of God's love deep within.

The second major mistake is the attempt to localize the Kingdom within one institution or one group or one place.

> Asked by the Pharisees when the kingdom of God was to come, he gave them this answer, "The coming of the kingdom of God does not admit of observation and there will be no one to say, 'Look, it is here! Look, it is there!' For look, the kingdom of God is among you." (Luke 17:20-21)

The temptation of all Churches is to think they are the gathering of the saved, the born-again elite ones, on the right side of the eternal border. Yet Jesus says the Kingdom of God is beyond clear observation. Like seasoning with salt or the action of leaven, it operates with invisible effect. No one possesses the Kingdom; it possesses you. You know you are merely a participant in a much larger mystery.

So Kingdom and Church are not the same thing. The Church is a means of pointing to the Kingdom of God, just as John the Baptist pointed toward the Lamb of God. When the Church does not point beyond itself to eternity and God, but only tries to make you loyal to the Church, it's entering into idolatry. Churches have done that in every age, and every Church I know does it. Now that doesn't mean we leave the Church; that means we need to have the humility to live in an imperfect world.

When you live in the Kingdom, you live in a "threshold space" between this world and the next. You learn how to live between heaven and earth, one foot in both worlds, holding them precious together. It will be a collision of opposites. If you try to hold those two worlds together you will pay for it in your body. That's why Jesus says if you're a Kingdom person be prepared for persecution, because the world wants to ask for all your loyalty. Jesus always answers the Pilates firmly but without rancor: "My kingdom is not of this world" (see John 18:36). That is the necessary *not-yet*.

In today's world, we are pressed to give our loyalty to the Stars and Stripes, to the navy, to General Motors or whatever company employs us. The Kingdom person can't do that anymore. That's what we mean by the Lordship of Jesus Christ: If God is Lord, then the other systems of this world do not exercise first or final voice in my decisions.

Non-Idolatry

If I had to summarize the social teaching of Jesus in one phrase it's the doctrine of non-idolatry. Don't idolize anything: even your marriage and your children are going to be taken from you. No form of government, no school of economics, no army or cause or country will ever be worth your whole soul. Serve God's world, but worship *nothing*. That is about as radical as you can get. Everything on earth is passing away. Spirituality is always about letting go. That's the rich, ultimate meaning of the word *forgiving*: handing it over before it is taken from us. We must fore-give all things.

There is no more radical teaching than the Kingdom. There are no more radical politics than the Kingdom. It makes relative every ideology, every loyalty, every addiction, every fascination, every attempt to affix our egos to this or to that. The Kingdom demands we recognize that all is passing away. It is the gate to perfect freedom. In the Kingdom we're free for God, free for the truth—even in this world. Kingdom people are the salt of the earth, preservatives of "something more." Like love, they make the world go round and keep the whole thing from self-destructing. Perhaps like Abraham's ten just ones (see Genesis 18:32), they maintain the world in existence.

A Two-Level Teaching

One finds a helpful and rather consistent pattern in the Synoptic Gospels: They usually address the same crowds on two levels at the same time. Whether you stand at the bottom or perceive yourself at the top, the Scriptures both challenge and console us all. This makes for a good Scripture study, and I recommend that you check it out for yourself.

In each situation, there seems to be a gospel for the oppressors and some good news for the oppressed, too. I suspect that we are all in both positions at different times and in different groupings, but in either case, we need liberation and truth. To those who have the power, the control, the answers, Jesus is always saying "Come down!" as he did to Zacchaeus, a wealthy senior tax collector. "Zacchaeus, come down. Hurry, because I am to stay at your house today" (Luke 19:5b-c). The issue quickly becomes one of justice and restitution. Many times, however, the elders and high priests and scribes refuse to "come down" from their judgments and their prepackaged conclusions. You can't fault Jesus for not trying, however.

The greatest number of people seem, instead, to be on the bottom: the sick, the outcasts, the indigent, the public sinners, the foreigners in a Jewish culture, the women in a patriarchal culture. To these Jesus' message is unrelenting and consistent: "Come up!" There are a number of one-liners from Jesus that did not win him many friends among the comfortable: "[Y]our faith has restored you to health; go in peace..." (Mark 5:34b); "[I]n no one in Israel have I found faith as great as this" (Matthew 8:10b); or "those now last...will be first, and those now first...will be last" (Luke 13:30). On both sides the reaction of "nice people" is outrage, scandal and sometimes even a plot to kill him.

I would interpret Jesus' strategy thus: If you have been at the bottom, he assumes that you might have learned the lessons of powerlessness and humility (done the First Step, as the Twelve-Step crowd would say!), and he is quite anxious for you to experience instead your dignity, goodness and inner power. He is always quite lavish and immediate with his affirmations—even without checking anyone's denominational affiliations or marital status. (Seems like there might just be a lesson hiding in there somewhere!)

But Jesus never courts the favor or patronage of those who are riding their high horse. His challenges are immediate and by our humanistic standards even harsh. I doubt whether we could or even should try the same method because we would then be jumping into the same saddle of superiority, but we must retrieve the prophetic level of the gospel. Ever since Constantine, the Church has been coddling the powers that be, hoping to win their favor for the new Catholic high school fund drive. Unfortunately, the gospel agenda does not influence the new high school nearly as much as the new high school determines what gospel we are even willing to consider. We have been in this dilemma for some centuries now, clergy and laity alike. Religious life was supposed to provide a way out, but now religious are often assimilated, too.

I always wondered why we had feast days and institutions named in honor of Christ the King, many statues and crosses of Christ the Priest, but I have never in all the Catholic world met a celebration or picture in honor of Christ the Prophet. Something's out of balance.

CHAPTER SEVEN

The Path of Transformation

No matter what religion or belief system people may hold to, underneath it all there are three possible worldviews. The universe is against us, the universe is for us, or the universe is neutral.

The latter says that reality is indifferent: It is neither for us nor against us. There is no God against us or for us; we're basically on our own in the universe. There are plenty of people in plenty of Churches who actually subscribe to this worldview. There probably is a God, and God might even be just and good, but this God is not actively involved in our lives or history. That worldview makes for very dead Churches.

You can be formally a Christian, Hindu, Buddhist or anything else and go through all the rites and services. But if the grace of God hasn't moved into the conscious and unconscious levels and really touched you—which is the full meaning of conversion—you can keep the formulas in your head but have no real awareness of the divine.

That's the malaise of Western Christianity today. People keep up the external observance of reliance upon God; underneath they depend only on themselves. "Nothing's going to happen unless I make it happen," they say to themselves. There is no active trust in the presence or the reality of God, or that God makes any real difference.

This form of secularism is malicious, because you can't get at it. All the right words and ideas are there—the person goes to Church, is born again or whatever—but beneath it all there is the sense of an indifferent universe and an indifferent, distant God.

Over the years I have been partially critical of the Charismatic movement, but I want to say something very good about it too.

Their "baptism in the Holy Spirit" was an experience of God actively involved in the world. I'm amazed how many people I meet today, in various social ministries throughout the country, who will reveal, sometimes after a beer at night, that they were in a prayer group some years ago. They say it almost as if they're ashamed. Yet for many people that experience helped them get the gospel out of their heads and into their guts. It seems unless Pentecost happens, most people remain in an indifferent universe. They have no active sense of God being a co-creator who is really involved in their daily lives.

If you stay in the indifferent universe for long, you usually move to the second worldview where people perceive reality as hostile, destructive or judgmental. Not only is God not involved but, in fact, God has to be appeased. There are plenty of people active in religion who are appeasing God. For those people God is somehow actively against us: watching us, judging us, critiquing us, certainly not on our side but making sure we jump the hoops, making sure that we win God's favor. Many Christians, even clergy and religious I've worked with over the years, don't want to believe that way, but it's clear that they do by the fearful way they live. They don't see God on their side, but almost as an opponent or nagging critic. It's probably highly symbolic that Pentecost comes fifty days after the sacramental experiences of Holy Thursday. You *can* be churched, or even ordained, and not believe that God is fire within you.

Most people's operative God image, in the early stages, is a combination of their mom and their dad, although most are unaware of it. Many of those who trust early and deeply in God had strong, nurturing parents. But if their dads were hostile, if their mothers were inconsistent or they felt they could not trust either one of them— basically that all gets transferred to God. Either way, child-parent relationships become foundations for our relationship with God.

Until you've moved to a level of prayer and surrender where God and grace are allowed to invade the subconscious—not just conscious— belief systems, it really doesn't matter in some ways what your conscious belief systems are. Until you get God into the subconscious where your deep agendas are touched and freed, your formal religion doesn't make a lot of difference. You can still have an indifferent, or even a hostile, destructive or judgmental worldview. It will show itself in fear, strong control needs, or the going through the motions that characterize an awful lot of churchgoers.

The third worldview can only be given by grace. It's given a great head start by loving, non-invasive parents who themselves believe in a benevolent universe. In this group the universe is not against me, nor is it sitting out there indifferent. Somehow it's even on my side. Reality can be trusted. I don't need to pull all the right strings or push all the right buttons; grace is everywhere. It's good to be here. Life is perhaps even difficult, but it is still good and trustworthy at the core.

Carl Jung speaks of synchronicity, Christianity speaks of providence, Hinduism speak of karma. Somehow they're all talking about a benevolent universe in which the foundation of all things is love. No matter how tragic things get, love can be trusted; you're standing in a solid universe. God is in charge and this God is good and involved. Pentecost has happened, just as with Jesus in the desert.

Until you meet a benevolent God and a benevolent universe, until you realize that the foundation of all is love, you will not be at home in this world. That meeting of God, that understanding experience cannot be communicated by words. You either have it or you don't. It is a gift of participation in the very life of God. Its inherent character is best described by three overlapping characteristics: faith, hope and love. We rightly called them the supernatural virtues because they were a "participation in the very life of God" as opposed to a natural talent.

In the early chapters of Matthew, Mark and Luke, Jesus undergoes a conversion. He is baptized, then goes to the desert. We don't know what happened to Jesus in the desert, but he comes out obviously believing in a loving universe that can be trusted. His insight is summarized in that wonderful phrase, "You are my beloved Son." The experience of being a beloved son (or daughter) is the experience of living in a loving universe: I am beloved, I am taken care of, I am believed in.

Anxiety is what reveals our real belief system. If you're

anxious—if you're worried about many things, to use Jesus' phrase (Matthew 6:25-34 counsels against worry five times!)—then you're still in one of the first two universes. If God isn't on your side, you've got to fix and control your world. Who else is going to? Why wouldn't you? Many people's religion is an obsession with security—and not just economic security: security of reputation, status, image. If you are still securing yourself or using religion to maintain or justify the self, your operative image of God is still an indifferent or hostile God. Don't be anxious about that either! We all start there, and the love-trust relationship grows over time.

Jesus' Definition of Faith

If you are a priest, you'll meet someone in an airplane who will invariably throw out this phrase: "Oh, don't get me wrong, Father. I believe in God." But that's not my concern. That's not what Jesus is concerned about. Belief in God is the primordial tradition since the beginning of time. Ninety-nine point nine percent of people who have ever lived on this earth have believed in God. Atheism is a modern rational phenomenon of the Western world that is a little blip on the screen. Of course there's a God! That's not even worth wasting time on! Faith, for Jesus, is *not* the opposite of not believing in God.

After assuring you that they believe in God, people on airplanes will add, "Well, I try to be good.... Now I don't go to church very much." Frankly, I don't think Jesus would really care. Going to church is not the issue either.

For Jesus, faith is not opposed to not believing in God, it doesn't mean you go to church, or that you're into religion or that you say "Lord, Lord!" (see Matthew 7:21). Faith for Jesus is *the opposite of anxiety*. If you are anxious, if you are trying to control everything, if you are worried about many things, you don't have faith, according to Jesus. You do not trust that God is good and on your side. You're trying to do it all yourself, lift yourself up by your own bootstraps.

The giveaway is *control*. That's a good litmus test of the quality of your faith. People of faith don't have to control everything, nor do they have to change people. You have the wisdom to know the difference, as the Twelve-Step people say. You cannot "fix" the soul. "Set your hearts on his kingdom first, and on God's saving justice, and all these other things will be given you as well. So do not worry about tomorrow: tomorrow will take care of itself" (Matthew 6:33-34a).

I usually say that if people are humble and honest, I really know they will be all right. If either humility or honesty is missing you've got some spiritual work to do. Of course we can grow in humility and grow in honesty, but if the seed is there, grace is going to keep invading you and breaking through. God is for you more than you are for yourself. And all you can do is be open. The One who created you cares like a parent for a child (see Isaiah 49:15). God cares for creation in an irrational way, a way that has nothing to do with logic, worthiness or correct behavior. We are cared for simply because we are beloved daughters and beloved sons. Paul expresses the same truth with the concepts of birthright and inheritance (Romans 8:14-17; Galatians 4:5-7; Ephesians 1:14). John simply describes it as the divine choice for our friendship, not our servitude (John 15:15-16).

Three Themes of Jesus

Three consistent themes recur in Jesus' teaching. (I'm relying here on the scholarship of Marcus Borg in his wonderful book, *Jesus: A New Vision*.) The first is *a new image of reality that challenges conventional wisdom*. I hope the whole of this book is an assault on that conventional wisdom. Jesus seems to think it is this very "normalcy" that keeps people from the banquet more than the so-called "hot sins"!

Conventional wisdom crucified Jesus. Then, as now, it was conventional wisdom that kept people from God. We think of wicked vices as keeping people from God, and indulging a vice certainly does. But people into the hot sins are often the ones who really hunger and thirst for justice. In the Gospels, these are the people who really seem to come around and get the truth. But the conventional wisdom people, who are trying to control it all and trying to be nice and proper, don't realize that they need to hunger and thirst for anything.

I believe that's the meaning of the "sin against the Holy Spirit" that Jesus says cannot be forgiven (see Matthew 12:32). The reason it cannot be forgiven is that it would never enter your mind that you have anything that needs to be forgiven! There's no asking for forgiveness, no recognition of being trapped. Conventional wisdom—status-quo culture that refuses to "turn around"—assures the group that they're elite, correct, the norm, that they do it well and swell.

Jesus talks about the broad way and the narrow way in Matthew 7:13-14. The broad way is conventional wisdom, I believe: the groupthink, cultural mood, collective sleepwalking that many take and that leads to destruction. Jesus describes the narrow gate, conversely, as a rough road that few discover, but that "leads to life"—obviously not conventional wisdom.

Jesus' second theme, to use a medical term, is *a diagnosis of the human condition*. Jesus is just describing what it means to be a human being, what all people are up against. Notice, to say *diagnosis* is not to say an answer (although Jesus finally *lives* an answer). Human life is a path, and the path will be partially death and partially joyous life. Trust the path. Let it unfold and see God in it. The human condition has an essentially tragic character that logic, riches or even science will never be able to erase. The same is true for happiness, which Jesus defines in a totally extraordinary way in Matthew 5:1-12 (as we will see in the next chapter). Jesus is content, it seems, to *describe* the human dilemma with insight, patience and compassion. Somehow that feels like an answer. It is.

The third consistent theme of Jesus is a description of *how transformation happens*, both for the person and for society. We have not been very good students of Jesus concerning personal transformation, emphasizing instead a kind of stoic "grin and bear it." As you would therefore expect, our teaching on transformation of institutions, structures and society has been even worse. Not ready for his doctrine of non-idolatry, we have sequentially put all our hope in the Roman Empire's favor, feudal lords, the divine right of kings, European culture, anti-Communism and democracy. I think the last one is about to disappoint us, too.

Transformation, though, is not the same as change. Change is when something new begins. Transformation is just the opposite. It more often than not happens when something old falls away. It happens after a crisis, when something we've learned to depend upon is taken away. Not all crises, of course, lead to transformation. When something is taken away that you've grown used to or addicted to, you will either turn bitter or be transformed.

Anyone reading this book has lived in a period of human history which has seen more change than any other century ever. We've undergone psychological change, cultural change, political change, economic change, worldview changes. Most people throughout history (except during times of plagues or violent upheavals) have lived their life inside one paradigm or model. Most people agreed upon one worldview. Yet there have been major paradigm shifts maybe four or five times during this century! Maybe that's why we have so many unhealthy people now. There has been massive change, but the change has not always been accompanied by transformation.

When change unaccompanied by the transformation of the soul is demanded, people are often destroyed. To be honest, most people don't age very well. Transformation is required to understand the changes that life asks of us, to resituate ourselves in the world. The function of all mythologies, stories and religion is to hold together your life in a meaningful universe. Every culture has both its creation stories and its story of the final end where all is tending. As Christians, we have the creation story of Genesis and the second coming of Christ as the Omega point.

These stories, usually picked up by osmosis in a healthy family and in healthy religion, situate us inside of a safe and meaningful universe. Just as the body needs food, so the soul needs meaning, and the spirit needs ultimate meaning. Some have called this "the cosmic egg" inside of which people can find rest and even happiness. Unless we know where it all came from and where it is all going, we tend to be anxious, incoherent and changing with the weathervane. This is the burden of modern secularism, and I'm sure the source of much mental and emotional illness in our society. As Jean Houston has said, "without mythology all we have left is our private pathology." For much of the post-modern world, the cosmic egg has not just cracked, it is gone altogether. In fact, many would deny any universal meanings or patterns. *The* story does not exist, all we can do is create our own moments of significance and meaning. It is all pretty fragile, as is the modern self.

Because this is so lonely and probably impossible, many at least move to a second level of "our" story. At least we can find value and meaning in our communal identities—our nationality, our ethnicity, our religion, our club or motorcycle gang. This takes away some of our private anxiety, but it is interesting how even group identities have moved in the direction of pathology. Support groups for everything from gamblers anonymous to survivors of breast cancer to parents of children who eat too much now fill our church basements. Some say that they gather more people than the Church proper. At any rate, *our story* is surely worthwhile, and we are grateful that people are discovering some language of community and interdependence. On the downside, it is also at the basis of gangs, militias, ethnic violence throughout the world and a lot of psychobabble that is going nowhere.

In general, one could say that many sophisticated, educated and progressive types tend to get trapped in the language of "my story," whereas many conservative and group-think folks tend to get trapped in "our story." The first become individualists because that is their first and final language: what *I* feel or think. The second become ideologues: loving explanations more than concrete people. Both are a clear avoidance of *the story*, what Jesus would call the Reign of God, the world of right relationships.

Again, the inclusive and holistic nature of the Reign of God is that it not only includes my story and our story, but actually demands that we take them both seriously—because God does. Thus the private journey and the collective history of Israel make up the Bible. For us theology and anthropology are the same thing. *The story* builds upon *my* personal experience and *our* historical experience as a people and gives us the only language by which we can understand the great and eternal patterns.

The Bible is not a listing of clear spiritual conclusions, although we would surely like that now and then. The Bible, instead, is a "text in travail" which invites us into the tension and journey itself. The Bible is a recorded history of what happens to human beings when they meet the True Sacred, the ways they avoid and deny Transcendence, and all the ways that we flirt with false transcendence. Jump in, it says, and then you will know the Bible is inspired because the patterns are yours too. You will not believe most of it by faith but by experience. Hear the phrase in a new way now: "the Bible is *always* true."

The Bible reveals patterns of truth, however, that are from beyond the pale. They are not the patterns that cultures of money, power or religion will naturally perceive. It seems they have to break in or "be revealed" from outside the system. These "pattern stories" become very explicit in the teaching of Jesus, although in most cases he is building upon his Jewish roots. He tries to make visible and explicit the patterns that are already there, but that we can't see. No wonder that he seems like a total traditionalist and a wild reformer at the same time. We find this creative tension is itself "the path of transformation." A Spirit-led person always knows how to put the two together, whereas tiny minds and hearts fall into cracks on either side. Let's list four of the big patterns, the "great themes" as I called them in my early audiocassettes in the 1970's (see diagram on the following page). These stories make up *The* story that is always true (but doesn't look true before you have walked it).

The Great Themes

1) **Exodus and Easter:** Life and death is the unavoidable pattern of growth and transformation. It is redemptive when trusted as God's way. It is the "only" sign Jesus says he will give: the sign of Jonah, the Paschal Mystery, the folly of the cross, exile and return.

2) **A bias toward the bottom:** Starting with enslaved Semites, then choosing the barren, the old, the last son, the rejected, the alien, the outcast, the sinner, the victim Jesus, the Bible reverses all human expectation.

3) **No correlation between gifts and worthiness:** With great and continuing difficulty, the Bible moves the focus from attainment to acceptance, from hard work to soft surrender, from "I am worthy" to "God is good." All is gratuitous. This fights all self-centered logic.

4) **Letting go:**

   - I will deliver you. "You have only to keep still" (Exodus 14:14). This becomes the faith theme throughout the Bible (*letting go of control*).

   - "Do not be afraid" is the most frequent line in the Bible (*letting go of fear*).

   - Yahweh your God will be your strength. "Cut off from me you can do nothing" (John 15:5) (*letting go of the small self*).

   - Most of Jesus' teaching is about one thing: forgiveness, which is the great and necessary thaw of all human history (*letting go of hurts*).

Thus we are taught that the path of transformation is very different than we might have imagined. It is not a language of ascent that the Bible gives us, not a search for spiritual superiority, not a disciplined attainment of higher states of consciousness ("Gnosticism" is a heresy that has been condemned in every century in a new form!), but exactly the opposite. The Bible gives us a language of descent, a search for who we already are, a releasing into an ordinary—and already extraordinary—humanity.

Our ordinary lives are given an extraordinary significance when we accept that our lives are about something much larger, our pain is a participation in the redemptive suffering of God, our creativity is the very passion of God for the world. No longer do we need to self-validate, self-congratulate or self-doubt—our place in the cosmos is assured. I do not need to be the whole play or even understand the full script. It is enough to know that I have been chosen to be one actor on the stage. I need only play my part as well as I can.

Did you know that the word *disaster* comes from the Latin word meaning "to be disconnected from the stars"? The stars represented the great story, the universal story. Our lives are usually a disaster unless we live under these stars. We live our little story under the great story. As long as you know that your little story—your little life of getting married and having children and dying in Omaha, Nebraska—as long as you know it's tied up to the big story you'll be sane and basically happy. Psychology and therapy cannot give you such a cosmology; only religion can.

What we have today in the West, as probably in no other time in human history, is the disconnection between our little stories and a great universal story. We don't believe the big story. We're lost in insignificance. Those of us who were raised in the old Catholic Church know it wasn't always that way. However you might criticize the Church before 1960, however you might think poorly of it now, it did something marvelous for most people. If you were raised well as a little Catholic girl or boy, you were told stories that tied you to a cosmic, coherent and compassionate universe!

I still remember sitting in the first grade, listening to Sister Charlotte Marie, a wonderful woman, telling us the story of Bethlehem. It's the story you and I hear every Christmas and see on countless Christmas cards. Think of how children listen to stories: with the mouth open in awe. To them it's all real. Then, as Christmas came, my parents would take me up to see the crib in the church and I could see it happening just as in the story. A child has no doubt that's what Mary and Joseph, Baby Jesus and the shepherds looked like. It's high drama and wonderful!

As January 6 approached they started marching the three kings across the sanctuary. We couldn't wait to get into the church on January 6. The shepherds would be gone and the three kings would be standing there. And that's exactly the way it was two thousand years ago, we thought. God came into the world: God was a little baby who's just like us with Mary, a loving mother, and Joseph, a loving father. The whole universe was rejoicing in his birth.

That's a benevolent universe. It's safe to live in this world. Jesus is poor but the world is still his chosen home. Now it is all right to be poor, to be human and to be *here*. "I think I'll live!" you might conclude. That's how religion, first of all *saves us*.

Jesus starts his Sermon on the Mount talking about happiness (see Matthew 5:3-12). The people I know who are happy always have a simple belief system. It's very concrete, it's personal, and they don't refashion it every week according to the new polls or the culture mood. The happiest people alive usually believe one or two things *really well,* and base their whole life on that. Let's now look at these few happy secrets.

The Cosmic Egg

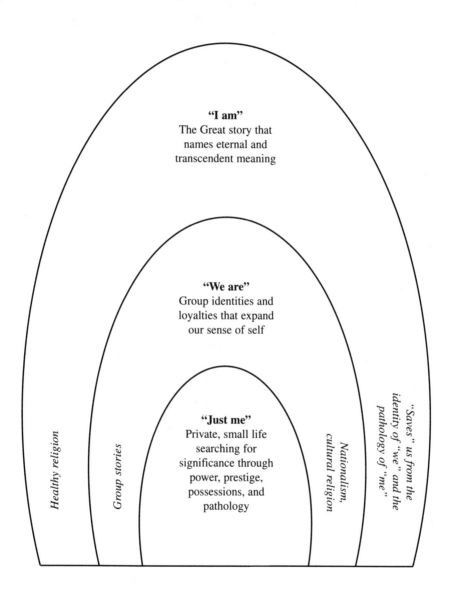

"I am"
The Great story that names eternal and transcendent meaning

"We are"
Group identities and loyalties that expand our sense of self

"Just me"
Private, small life searching for significance through power, prestige, possessions, and pathology

Healthy religion

Group stories

Nationalism, cultural religion

"Saves" us from the identity of "we" and the pathology of "me"

CHAPTER EIGHT

The 'Happy Attitudes,' Salt and Light

M atthew sets the stage for the Sermon with three simple sentences: "Seeing the crowds, he went onto the mountain. And when he was seated his disciples came to him. Then he began to speak" (5:1-2a). Remember Moses came down from the mountaintop. Matthew's message is clear: This is the new Moses going back to the mountaintop, reproclaiming the truth, bringing down the new law. That is a very important context: In a certain sense, the Sermon is the replacement of the Ten Commandments.

The "happy attitudes" ("congratulations" would be our secular equivalent) or Beatitudes, as we traditionally call them, are addressed not to the crowds, but to Jesus' disciples. That's a clue to how important the happy attitudes are. It's only the smaller group of disciples who are prepared to hear this challenging sermon. The heaviest stuff in the Gospel—"taking up the cross"—is addressed not to the crowds or the disciples, but to the inmost circle of the Twelve. The Sermon is addressed to the second circle of disciples, who are still being initiated. That's us!

There is a very real plan in Jesus' initiation, it seems. He is aware of timing, readiness and maturation. At the early stages you are not ready for the hard gospel; you can't hear the cross. I would say most people under thirty have a hard time understanding the cross because the ego is saying, "Grow, grow, grow; become, become, become." You can't walk into a twenty-one-year-old's life and say, "Die." Dying doesn't make sense to a young person. But something happens to us as we grow older. Some are in their thirties or forties when the truth starts sinking in: Dying is a part of life. By fifty or sixty we must learn that dying is not opposed to life; it's a part of a greater mystery—and we are a part of that mystery. The older psyche is ready to hear such sober truth.

'How blessed are the poor in spirit: the kingdom of Heaven is theirs' (Matthew 5:3)

What an opening line! I always say it's the opener of the inaugural address. "How happy are the poor in spirit." It's crucial, a key to everything Jesus is teaching, or it wouldn't be the opener. It is hard to imagine that a saying so radical should become so familiar, so normal. It does appear that Matthew has chosen to soften it from the more original phrase that we see in Luke and the noncanonical Gospel of Thomas (rediscovered in Naj Hammadi, Egypt, in 1945). You will find the more primitive Beatitudes in Luke 6:20-49. Luke's Gospel is for the poor, so he leaves the hard words of Jesus as they were originally spoken, the scholars say: "How blessed are you who are poor" (6:20a). The counterpoint is also listed: "But alas for you who are rich" (Luke 6:24a). There's no softening of things in Luke.

That's not to fault Matthew, smart man. He's got a nice middle-class community, folks who have good jobs in the business community or the defense labs, you know. He'd better not say *poor* or they'll walk out on the talk. So he says, "Happy are the poor in spirit." The truth is still there: Poor in spirit means to live without a need for your own righteousness. It's inner emptiness; no outer need for your own reputation. If you're poor in spirit it won't be long before you're poor. In other words, you won't waste the rest of your life trying to get rich because you'll know better.

There are a number of words describing the different states of poverty. New Testament scholars point out that the normal Greek word used for the peasant class is *tapeinoi*, but that is not the word Matthew and Luke use here. They use the word *ptochoi*, which would apply not to the eighty percent in the peasant class but to the eighth and ninth classes: the unclean and those who are expendable (see Chapter Four). *Ptochoi* literally means "the very empty ones, those who are crouching." They are the bent-over beggars, the little nobodies of this world who have nothing left. Jesus is saying:

130

"Happy are you, you're the freest of all." James, the "brother of Jesus," uses the same word in his letter: "...[I]t was those who were poor according to the world that God chose, to be rich in faith and to be the heirs to the kingdom which he promised to those who love him" (James 2:5b). Maybe they were taught such wisdom by their own family and life-style.

The higher up you are in the system the more trapped you are. The more you're outside the system, the freer you are. Everyone knows that for every promotion or recognition you accept, there is a price: more party line! That is surely true for business and almost any organization, including the Church. There's a cynical joke among priests: "A bishop never gets two things—a bad meal or the truth."

The point is that when you're high up in anything, you are expected to represent it, hold it together and affirm it! Why not? You would likely be irresponsible if you didn't. So the spiritual greats, like Jesus, just say, "Avoid it!" When we go to a party, most of us want to be slapped on the back by the gang, to be a part of the old boy network (and there is an old girl network, too, by the way!). It's not that people who want to be accepted are *bad*. It's just that you like Chris to like you, so you tend to say what Chris wants you to say. The price of the truth can be very great. We say what is needed to survive and to be liked inside the group, and to hold the group in unity.

"How blessed are the poor in spirit" (Matthew 5:3a), the little ones who don't have to play any of these games. Jesus is recommending a social reordering here, quite different from common practice. Notice how he also uses present tense: "The kingdom of heaven *is* theirs" (Matthew 5:3b, emphasis added). He doesn't say "theirs *will* be...." That tells us, once again, that the Kingdom isn't later. It's present tense: You *are* the free ones now, if you remain without anything to protect or anything you need to prove or defend.

I know people who have left Christianity to become Buddhists precisely because of the doctrines of emptiness, simplicity and nonviolence that they discovered in Buddhist teaching. If only they had been taught these same foundations in Jesus' Beatitudes!

'Blessed are *the gentle: they shall have the earth as inheritance'* (Matthew 5:4)

This Beatitude is a quote from Psalm 37:11: "the humble shall have the land for their own." Some translate it "the nonviolent." The translation perhaps most familiar is "the meek." There's irony here. If there was one hated group in Palestine of Jesus' day, it was landlords, those who possess the land. Nobody possessed land except by violence, by oppression, by holding onto it and making all the little peasants pay a portion of their harvest. Jesus is turning that around and saying no, it's you little ones who are finally going to possess the land. It's said with sarcasm, with irony, but with hope.

Jesus is undoubtedly redefining the meaning of land, building on what every Jew would have known. Hebrew Scripture teaches that only God possesses the land (see Psalm 24:1; Leviticus 25:23). In the jubilee year, all the land was to be given back to its original occupants (see Leviticus 25:8-17). The Native Americans understood the freedom of the land, yet Western society cannot. Private property forces us behind fences, boundaries and walls. We actually think that we "own" the land because there's a deed down at the courthouse. Isn't that strange? It's all cultural. People closer to the earth know that only God possesses the earth, that we're all stewards, pilgrims and strangers on the earth.

Possession is an illusion in the light of the Kingdom. What do you possess? Wait a few years—we'll see how much you possess when you're six feet under! You don't *possess* anything. But that's ridiculous talk unless you understand *the* story. Once you understand *the* story you know that possession is a passing illusion. The meek know that landlords, flood or drought can quickly take the land back.

This image of meekness is the one Saint Francis embraced. He told us never to own anything so that you can be open to everything. There is a strain of this thinking in the American tradition of free public libraries and art museums. I don't have to buy art and bring it home to my house to possess it. It's everywhere, all around us. Personal ownership is not necessary for enjoyment. Why can't it be everybody's sculpture or painting? And why can't it be in a common place where we all can look at it?

In most areas of our lives, though, we think that we have to bring things into our homes to possess them. After a while, your things possess you.

'Blessed are those who mourn: they shall be comforted' (Matthew 5:5)

On men's retreats we speak of grief work. There is a therapeutic, healing meaning to tears. Undoubtedly that's true, even as we study what's in tears. We speak of salt in tears but now there's evidence of washed-out toxins. Is not weeping, in fact, necessary? Beyond that, of course, Jesus is describing the state of those who weep, who have something to mourn about. They feel the pain of the world. Jesus is saying that those who can grieve, those who can cry are those who will understand.

The Syrian Fathers Ephraim and Simeon weren't as popular as the Greek Fathers in the early centuries of the Church. The Greek Fathers tended to filter the gospel through the head; the Syrians' theology—like a lot of the present feminist theology—is much more localized in the body. The Syrian Fathers, in effect, wanted tears to be a sacrament in the Church. Saint Ephraim goes so far as to say until you have cried you don't know God. How different!

We think we know God through ideas. Yet corporeal theology, body theology, says weeping perhaps will allow you to know God much better than ideas. In this Beatitude, Jesus praises the weeping class, those who can enter into solidarity with the pain of the world and not try to extract themselves from it. That is why Jesus says the rich man can't see the Kingdom. The rich one spends life trying to make tears unnecessary and, ultimately, impossible. Weeping over our sin and the sin of the world is an entirely different mode than self-hatred or hatred of others. The weeping mode, if I can call it that, allows one to carry the dark side, to bear the pain of the world without looking for perpetrators or victims, but instead recognizing the tragic reality that both sides are caught up in. Tears from God are always *for everybody*, for our universal exile from home. "It is Rachel weeping for her children,/refusing to be comforted..." (Jeremiah 31:15b).

That seems ridiculous, and it is especially a stumbling block to men in our culture. To men's groups I say that the young man who cannot cry is a savage; the old man who cannot laugh is a fool. But something in our culture has told young men not to cry. That will make us look vulnerable. So we men stuff our tears. We die, by the way, an average of many years earlier than women. Could there be a connection? It seems likely. We must teach all young people how to cry. In the second half of my life I understand why Saints Francis and Clare cried so much, and why the saints spoke of "the gift of tears."

'Blessed are those who hunger and thirst for justice: they shall have their fill' (Matthew 5:6)

Most Bibles to this day will soften this Beatitude: "hunger and thirst for what is right" or "for righteousness" are the more common translations. That's a softer, more religious, message. The word in Greek clearly means "justice." Notice that the concept of justice is exactly halfway through the Beatitudes and at the very end again. It's a couplet saying, This is the point: To live a just life in this world is to have identified with the longings and hungers of the poor, the meek and those who weep. This identification and solidarity is already a profound form of social justice. This Beatitude is surely both spiritual *and* social.

Much as Matthew tries to soften it for his middle-class audience, he really can't soften Jesus' central message. It's still unsettling and most extraordinary. "Make sure you're not satisfied" is the message. "Keep yourself in a state of deliberate dissatisfaction." Contemplatives know this. In contemplation you can't always say you've met God, or that you've come to some great insight after praying. What real prayer does is stir holy desire but not always satisfy it. As the unconscious bubbles up, you find out what it is you really desire. First you move through the layers of superficial desire. Both addiction counselors and spiritual directors will tell you that when you respond to a need with a substitute it only intensifies the need.

At first, it might be a new house, a new set of clothes, a new image that you think you desire. You might think that by getting a new set of clothes you're going to be happy. Stay with it longer. It's not a new set of clothes. Prayer will move you to the primary level where you find out *what you really desire*: It's always God. It's always union, love, communion. "Our hearts are restless until they rest in God," is how Saint Augustine said it. The sad thing about those who refuse to accept that state of longing and thirsting is that they are never satisfied anyway. Even the wealthiest person is never satisfied. The very character of greed is that it is insatiable. It needs an ever-higher dosage to achieve the old satisfaction. When you get more, it still doesn't satisfy. Jesus says, "Why not go the exact opposite direction? Directly and positively choose emptiness until it loses its terror."

In all my years as a Catholic priest hearing confessions, I've never had anybody confess violating the Tenth Commandment: coveting their neighbor's goods. Yet coveting goods is what our entire culture is built on! Billboards and advertisements create desire after desire. Salesmanship, the creating of false need through advertising and marketing, is the only game in town. I've also never had an American Christian seriously question the goal of increasing or maximizing profits.

When I first preached in the former Communist world, in eastern Germany, the most striking thing was to be in a world without any billboards or other advertisements. I didn't realize how much we're surrounded by it. A newspaper without a single advertisement is incredibly shorter that what we are accustomed to. We don't realize how much our world is controlled by created desires for things we do not need or really want. To quote Paul in a new context: "Who will rescue me from this body doomed to death?" (Romans 7:24b).

Two practical suggestions that friends have shared with me for overcoming covetousness: One friend simply refuses to read or even look at *any* magazine or newspaper advertisements, even to check for sales or better prices. It only keeps us preoccupied with the whole game. Let's fast from advertising!

Another friend told me that when he found himself *upset* because he had been ripped off, lost money, made a bad money choice or the like, he now had the policy of giving that very amount he lost to charity! Reverse double-dipping, you could call it. I

needed for him to repeat it to me because my German save-a-penny
attitude went into shock. That's probably how Jesus' hearers
responded to him!

'Blessed are the merciful: they shall have mercy shown them' (Matthew 5:7)

Mercy is like the mystery of forgiveness. By definition, mercy
and forgiveness are unearned, undeserved, not owed. If it isn't all
those three, it won't be experienced as mercy. If you think people
have to be merciful, or, on the other hand, try to earn mercy, you've
lost the mystery of mercy and forgiveness. *I believe with all my
heart that mercy and forgiveness are the whole gospel.*

The Benedictus (Luke 1:68-79) says you'll have knowledge of
salvation through the forgiveness of sin (1:77). The experience of
forgiveness or mercy is the experience of a magnanimous God who
loves out of total gratuitousness. There's no tit for tat, no buying
and selling in the Temple. That is the symbolism of Jesus kicking
over the tables: The buying and selling of God is over. One cannot
buy and sell God by worthiness, by achievement, by obeying
commandments. Salvation is God's loving-kindness, a loving-
kindness that is "forever." Read Psalm 136 for an ecstatic
description.

You don't know mercy until you've really needed it. As
Thomas Merton once said—and I've quoted it often—"Mercy
within mercy, within mercy." It's as if we collapse into deeper nets
of acceptance, deeper nets of being enclosed and finally find we're
in a net we can't fall out of. We are captured by grace. Only after
much mistrust and testing do we accept that we are accepted.

I once saw God's mercy as patient, benevolent tolerance, a kind
of grudging forgiveness. But now mercy has become for me God's
very self-understanding, a loving allowing, a willing breaking of
the rules by the One who made the rules—a wink and a smile, a
firm and joyful taking of our hand while we clutch at our sins and
gaze at God in desire and disbelief. So many things have now
become signs for me of this abundant mercy, not grudgingly
extended, but patiently offered—to this Church, to this age, to each
of us. As we grow older, it almost takes more and more humility to

receive the mercy of God.

Mercy is a way to describe the mystery of forgiveness. More than a description of something God does now and then, it is who-God-is. According to Jesus, "Mercy is what pleases me, not sacrifice" (Matthew 9:13; 12:7). The word is *hesed* in Hebrew, "the steadfast enduring love which is unbreakable." Sometimes the word is translated as "loving-kindness" or "covenant love." God has made a covenant with creation and will never break the divine side of the covenant. It's only broken from our side. God's love is steadfast. It is written in the divine image within us. It's given, it sits there. We are the ones who instead clutch at our sins and beat ourselves instead of surrendering to the divine mercy. That refusal to be forgiven is a form of pride. It is saying, "I'm better than mercy. I'm only going to accept it when I'm worthy and can preserve my so-called self-esteem." Only the humble person, the little one, can live *in* and *after* mercy.

The mystery of forgiveness is God's ultimate entry into powerlessness. Look at the times when you have withheld forgiveness. It's always your final attempt to hold a claim over the one you won't forgive. It's the way we finally hold onto power, to seek the moral high ground over another person. I will hold you in unforgiveness, and you're going to know it just by my coldness, by my not looking over there, by my refusal to smile, or whatever. Oh, we do it subtly to maintain our sense of superiority. Non-forgiveness is a form of power over another person, a way to manipulate, shame, control and diminish another. God in Jesus refuses all such power.

If Jesus is the revelation of what is going on inside the eternal God (see Colossians 1:15), which is the core of Christian faith, then we are forced to conclude that God is very humble. That is amazing, difficult to imagine. Sometimes I think I could just stop and meditate on that for the rest of my life. This God seems never to hold rightful claims against us. Abdicating what we thought was the proper role of God, this God "has thrust all my sins behind his back" (see Isaiah 38:17b).

We do not attain anything by our own holiness but by ten thousand surrenders to mercy. A lifetime of received forgiveness allows you to *become* mercy: That's the Beatitude. You become forgiveness because it's the only thing that makes sense to you, the only thing that's alive within you. Mercy becomes your energy, your meaning. Perhaps we are finally enlightened and free when we can both receive it and give it away—without payment or punishment.

Meditate, if you will, on this frontispiece I wrote for my book *Near Occasions of Grace*:

> When grace is a punishment for you, you are in Hell.
> When grace and punishment are fighting within you,
> you are in Purgatory.
> When grace is received without payment or
> punishment, you are in Heaven.

'Blessed are the pure in heart: they shall see God' (Matthew 5:8)

When the heart is right, seeing will be right, Jesus says. He ties together heart and sight. Consider the saying, "Beauty is in the eyes of the beholder." So is God. All we need do is keep the lens clean. If your heart is cold, your vision is distorted. Perhaps you don't like someone; you want to hurt her because she hurt you. You want to make him feel bad, to let him know that he hurt you. If there is coldness and unforgiveness or the desire to do violence verbally, or just to avert your loving gaze so that another person will feel your rejection, you will not be able to see clearly. The heart is not pure.

Jesus says, "The lamp of your body is your eye. When your eye is clear, your whole body, too, is filled with light; but when it is diseased your body, too, will be darkened" (Luke 11:34). What you always see in people who love God and themselves is the ability to make eye contact. When you hate yourself, you cannot look someone else in the eye. People who do not know God or love will hate themselves and doubt the divine image within themselves. They shut you out, perhaps, because they are afraid you will not see it there, either.

In my work as a jail chaplain, I've found it's the hardest thing to get the inmates to look at me eyeball to eyeball. They always put their heads down. There seems to be a terrible sense of failure and inferiority. You want to hold up their heads sometimes and say,

"Look at me. Don't you know you're a son of God, a beloved daughter?" But they close their eyelids as if to say, "Just don't look in here." There's too much power in the eye, too much power given and received. It might heal, it might change us, we might have to believe it. Truth comes through the eyes: It's very hard to lie with your eyes.

So Jesus calls us to purity of heart with the promise that correct seeing will follow, but in other places he also says the opposite is true: pure seeing will give us bright hearts.

'Blessed are the peacemakers: they shall be recognized as children of God' (Matthew 5:9)

This is the only time the word *peacemakers* is ever used in the whole Bible. A peacemaker literally is the "one who reconciles quarrels." Clearly you can see Jesus is not on the side of the violent but on the side of the nonviolent. Jesus is saying there must be a connection, a clear consistency, a constant unity between means and ends. There is no way to peace other than peacemaking itself.

Today many think we can achieve peace through violence. Have you ever heard them say, "We will stop killing by killing"? Of course you have. It's the way we think and it is in opposition to all great religious teachers. Our need for immediate control leads us to disconnect the clear unity between means and ends. We even name a missile that is clearly meant for the destruction of humanity a "peacekeeper." At least the word is more honest: *peace keeper*, instead of Jesus' *peace maker*. But the peace we are keeping is a false peace. Jeremiah the prophet would say to our "peacekeeping" wars what he said to the leaders of Israel:

...Peace! Peace!
whereas there is no peace.
They should be ashamed of their loathsome deeds.
Not they! They feel no shame,
they do not even know how to blush.
(Jeremiah 8:11b-12a)

American Christians supported the killing of two hundred thousand people in Iraq during the Persian Gulf War and still dare to call themselves pro-life.

War is a means of seeking *control*, not a means of seeking peace. *Pax Romana* is the world's way of seeking control and calling it peace. In ancient Rome all the Romans thought they had peace. They lived in the city of Rome and everything seemed OK. Violence, you see, will always create more violence, but it creates the violence at the edge, out in the colonies. It calls what it has at the center peace, yet the violence has merely been exported to the edges. It is no real peace. Our rich suburbs with security entrances are evidence of the same today. "There is no true peace," as Paul VI said, "without justice."

Do we have any idea of all the slavery and oppression, all the killing, the torture, all the millions of people who have existed around the edges of every empire so those at the center of the empire could say they had peace? Every time you build a pyramid, certain people at the top will have their peace. Yet there will be bloody bodies all around the bottom. Those at the top are usually blind to the price of their false peace.

But in the Sermon, Jesus defines peace in a different way. We call this the *Pax Christi*, the peace of Christ. In the remaining Beatitudes Jesus will connect his peace with justice and self-sacrifice. The *Pax Romana* creates a false peace by sacrificing others; the *Pax Christi* waits and works for true peace by sacrificing the false self of power, prestige and possessions. That will never become national policy of any country. It is unlikely to be espoused by any political party of any country at any time. Neither will such peacemaking ever be popular. The follower of Jesus is doomed to perennial minority status.

Jesus next warns us that we will be hated from all sides (see also John 15:18—16:2 or Matthew 10:22). When you're working outside the system, when you work for peace you will not be admired inside the system. In fact you will look dangerous, subversive, unpatriotic and all the other things that people's fears will create. They used to call us Communists; now they're searching for a new word to call us. One thing you cannot call Jesus was a patriot. He was naming a far bigger world.

If you are truly pro-life, your very means have to be nonviolent and you have to be consistently pro-life—from womb to tomb. One of the most distressing qualities of Christians today is that they retain the right to decide when, where and with whom they will be pro-life peacemakers. At the extreme end, if the other can be determined to be wrong, guilty, unworthy, sinful or "not innocent" in any way, it is apparently acceptable to kill them. That entirely misses the ethical point that Jesus is making: We are *never* the sole arbiters of life or death, because life is created by God and carries the divine image. Why can't so-called conservatives and fundamentalists be strict about that! It is a *spiritual seeing*, far beyond any ideology of left, right or even Church.

Each year on the feast of John the Baptist, some of my coworkers and I take a vow of nonviolence. We know that we will never fully live up to it. Like any vow, it has to first find a home in the heart so that eventually we can live it in the outer world.

'Blessed are those who are persecuted in the cause of justice: the kingdom of Heaven is theirs' (Matthew 5:10)

I guess we should not be surprised that this Beatitude follows the previous ones. The first and the last Beatitudes are present tense: Theirs *is* the Kingdom of heaven. Also, up until now Jesus has said happy "the...," talking generally. Now he says happy "those of you...." Very likely he's talking about what's going on right in front of him. Persecution has begun to happen to the believing community, and he's telling them to "rejoice and be glad"! Persecution for the cause of justice is inevitable. Instead of seeking to blame someone for their well-earned scars, he is telling them two clear things: You can be *happy—now*! Try living *that* in a country of lawyers and litigation.

One cannot help but wonder if an action that was motivated by conscience or the gospel could ever be vindicated by whining, blaming or suing. Perhaps all our lawsuits are, in fact, a recognition that the self we are defending is very fragile, insecure and afraid. The self that Jesus proclaims is so grounded that it can consider persecution an asset.

'Rejoice and be glad...' (Matthew 5:12a)

Matthew 5:11-12 could really be called the ninth Beatitude, although it more likely is an explanation of the eighth:

> Blessed are you when people abuse you and persecute you and speak all kinds of calumny against you falsely on my account. Rejoice and be glad, for your reward will be great in heaven; this is how they persecuted the prophets before you.

Apparently Jesus is saying that the disciples' response is a *prophetic* action itself. To live joyfully in the midst of misunderstanding and persecution points beyond to *the* story. Jesus promises us that when we do live joyfully under persecution, the world won't understand, it will hate you. Many before me have said that a clear sign that it *is* true gospel is if it engenders criticism and spreading of falsehoods ("calumny"). Goodness can never be attacked directly; the messengers or the motivation have to be discredited.

Luke's Gospel presents the same message in exactly the opposite form: "Alas for you when the world speaks *well* of you! This was the way their ancestors treated the *false* prophets" (Luke 6:26, emphases added). Too much praise is probably an indication that it is *not* the full gospel. In either case, Jesus himself clearly knew that his teaching would turn conventional values on their head.

Who Will Preserve the Essentials?

Jesus says that those who live these happinesses, these Beatitudes, such people will be "the salt of the earth" (see Matthew 5:13). What does he mean by such an image?

First of all, he's *not* saying that those who live this way are going to heaven. He is saying that they will be a certain kind of gift for the *earth*. What a misinterpretation has been handed on again and again! We think of Jesus' teaching as a set of *prescriptions* for getting to heaven (even though we haven't followed them). No, the Sermon on the Mount and especially the Beatitudes are a set of *descriptions* of a free life. They are more than prescriptions, so don't even try to interpret them in the mode of law.

Jesus' moral teaching is very often a description of the final product rather than a detailed process for getting there. When you can weep, when you can identify with the little ones, when you can make peace, when you can be persecuted and still be joyful; then you're doing it right. He is saying, as it were, this is what holiness will look like. When you act this way, "the kingdom of God is among you" (Luke 17:21b). Jesus has low control needs, it seems. His concern is proclamation, naming, revealing, stating. Then he trusts that good-willed people and a reliable God will take it from there. Jesus is not concerned about enforcement or uniformity. What a shame that we can't do the same!

If salt becomes tasteless, how can we salt the world with it? asks Jesus (see Matthew 5:13). That message seems especially true today. If we no longer believe the gospel, if we no longer believe in nonviolence and powerlessness, then who's going to convert *us*? We're supposed to be the leaven of the world, yet if we no longer believe in the gospel, what hope do we have of offering anything new to the nations?

It seems so many saints and prophets who start out to preach to the world come back to convert or reconvert the People of God. Until the Church believes its own core message, there's no point in going out and telling other people to be Christian. There is no new world order to point to or to bring them home to. Jesus' conclusion is rather pessimistic compared to our practice of plugging along with an awful lot of "salt that has lost its zing." He says "it's good for nothing but to be thrown out and trampled underfoot." Wow!

By calling his disciples salt of the earth, he's not saying they're the saved ones. He never tries to create a "members-only" club. Jesus consistently says, in fact, that God loves those on the outside just as much as God loves the insiders; that there's just as much mercy *out* there as *in* there among Jesus' closest followers. If we don't believe our own message we're good for nothing. We do more harm than good.

Jesus is calling us to creative self-criticism and giving us the capacity for self-regeneration. As long as some people hold on to the upside-down wisdom of the gospel, it will be enough to flavor the whole meal of life. The Good News gives a taste to the world.

In short, it is not as important that each individual "gets saved" as it is that the gospel wisdom be in the world for *our* salvation. Western individualists have a hard time with that. Salt is tiny and invisible, but for ancient people it was the only preservative, the only spice, and often a symbol of healing.

Just Do It Better

Finally Jesus says, "You are light for the world. A city built on a hill-top cannot be hidden" (Matthew 5:14-15a). We used to say in the seminary, "That which is tottering need not be pushed." It's not real and it's going to fall apart anyway. So why waste your time getting mad at it? Why waste your time attacking it? Conversely, Jesus is saying here that the real cannot be destroyed—only ignored. The unreal will show itself as unreal in time. Our job is to be a shining truth, to live on the mountaintop, to live the truth as best we can and let it fall where it may. What a difficult and non-pushy way to live! "The best criticism of the bad is the practice of the better," has become a near-motto for me.

"In the same way your light must shine in people's sight, so that, seeing your good works, they may give praise to your Father in heaven" (Matthew 5:16). Jesus says "*your* Father" almost as a calm and secure assumption. He is seemingly trying to invite us into the same relationship with God that he has. He's not just *my* Father, Jesus is saying, but he's also yours. So we needn't be the mountaintop, the city, the whole house. We're simply that which shines on the mountaintop, which illuminates the house. We're not the whole loaf of bread, we're just the leaven. We're not the whole meal, we're not the broccoli, mashed potatoes or roast beef; we're just the salt, and our shared and loving God is the banquet, the mountain and the focus of all praise.

What modest images these are. I don't think Jesus ever expected the whole world to follow him. Obviously the world is not all going to become Christian. For the most part, the only people who are being converted to Christianity today are secular types and animists. Muslims, Hindus, Jews and Buddhists seldom become Christians anymore. The cultural barriers are too vast. Jesus is telling his disciples, "I've given you a great truth, I want you to hold the light and the leaven in the middle of the world. As light or leaven, it will do its work, and God's purposes will be achieved." What relaxed and patient trust Jesus has in God!

Although his images are very modest, they are also very hopeful. The Church has always been the most effective, I think, when it has been in a minority or even persecuted position. The Spirit works best underground, when we work from the bottom. Jesus surely never intended Christendom to be gospel imposed by law and government and majority status. God knows we've tried: We poured water over the Italians, the Germans, the Spanish, the French. But as soon as the Church became establishment, as soon as we came into power, we lost the true power, the effective virus of the gospel. Jesus says we are a mere mustard seed, we are leaven, we are the pearl of great price, we are a hidden treasure in the field.

Jesus is quite content, it seems, with such a humble position. He always enters the imperial city from a place of powerlessness. Our path, apparently, must be the same: "Do not be afraid, daughter of Zion; see your king is coming, mounted on a colt of a donkey" (see Zechariah 9:9).

The introductory teaching in the Sermon on the Mount all has to do with a new understanding and strategy of power. Jesus is leading us into the power that is apparently the power of God. To us it feels like powerlessness.

CHAPTER NINE

Bridges and Boundaries: Liberals and Conservatives

Do not imagine that I have come to abolish the Law or the Prophets. I have come not to abolish but to complete them. In truth I tell you, till heaven and earth disappear, not one dot, not one little stroke, is to disappear from the Law until all its purpose is achieved. Therefore, anyone who infringes even one of the least of these commandments and teaches others to do the same will be considered the least in the kingdom of Heaven; but the person who keeps them and teaches them will be considered great in the kingdom of Heaven. (Matthew 5:17-20)

Notice how Jesus now leads into his teaching on the Law: "I have not come to abolish the Law" (Cool it, liberals!); the Law will not disappear "until its purpose is achieved" (Beware, mindless legalists!); "Your virtue must go deeper than the scribes and Pharisees or you will never enter the kingdom" (It's about Kingdom values and depth, not just external behavior.)

Here we have the balance Jesus strikes between what we call conservative and liberal. He holds onto the foundation and center of the old, while moving the boundaries out much farther than almost anyone expected. On a continuum between inclusiveness and exclusiveness, we see that Jesus is trying to find a delicate balance. Exclusivity at its extreme would have been the Law of Holiness (Leviticus 17—25). Such an exclusive approach to Law can mean petrification, solidification, isolation and irrelevance. That's true in any group when boundaries between insiders and outsiders become overemphasized. But it also gives a people a strong and often psychologically healthy sense of identity and boundaries. We surely could use that today.

But inclusivity at its extreme, where all the boundaries are thrown out and "everything is beautiful," as the liberal type wants to say, very often can mean standing for nothing, betrayal of central and essential truths. That can eventually lead to disintegration of the group. Nothing enduring can be built when there's a refusal to stand for anything. After a while you ask the question, "Well, why belong?" It doesn't really matter because there's no real group identity. So liberals generally don't build anything enduring. Wisdom is knowing how to hold both inclusion and exclusion in ideal tension. We're going to see that Jesus is really a master at that.

Charles Williams (1886-1944), a brilliant Christian writer, describes this tension very well in *The Descent of the Dove* (Grand Rapids, Mich.: Eerdmans, 1974, 1939). He says "the rigorous view," what we are calling exclusivity, "is vital to sanctity; the relaxed view is vital to sanctity. Their union, however, is not impossible but it is difficult. For whichever is in power begins, after the first five minutes, to maintain itself from bad and unworthy motives. Harshness, pride, resentment encourage the one over the other."

On the side of exclusivity you might hear, "We are the true people who have got it." Williams's description of the possible sin on the other end is even more interesting. He calls it "indulgence, falsity, and detestable good fellowship," this need to feel good that often characterizes the liberal. On the side of inclusivity you might hear, "There are no real boundaries that I need to stand for because the all-important thing is that you like me and I like you." Abdication never leads to depth or integrity. If you don't believe in anything, you will fall for everything.

Williams is daring enough to say something that probably we wouldn't say today: "detestable good fellowship." But I get the point. If we're willing to betray the deeper self to feel good and manufacture cheap communion in the moment, in the long run we don't have anything enduring. Williams later concludes, "Our Lord the Spirit is reluctant to allow either of the *two great ways*—the rigorous way or the relaxed way—to flourish without courtesy to the other."

It reminds me of what I often say in spiritual direction to the more rigorous type, to those who are trying too hard to maintain self-image in one direction. I say, "Make sure you nod to your shadow each day." In other words, give yourself some gentle recognition that you are also lazy, ordinary, sensual—whatever it might be—because when you repress the shadow too rigorously it will always come out indirectly anyway. Everybody else can see it but you.

Further on, Jesus talks about not seeing the great log in your own eye, yet seeing the splinter in somebody else's (see Matthew 7:4). That, I think, is a marvelous description of the shadow. You must recognize the dark side within yourself: That leads you to the relaxed view. Once you see that what you hate *over* there is largely a projection of what's *in* here, an attempt to maintain yourself in superiority, then you can't be overly rigorous. Rigorism usually is tied up with a strong ability to repress what you don't want to see, the dark side.

On the other hand, the relaxed view sins not by repression but by too-quick *expression*! At both extremes, you lose the energy that teaches. Too-quick expression, too-quick consummation loses the real power of the moment, the creative insight, because you act on it before you have learned its lessons. That's really the meaning of celibacy, too. Healthy celibates learn how to live their loneliness until their erotic longings become the ultimate longing: the longing for God. It's the same with patience itself, poverty, silence, fasting, forgiveness, letting go and nonviolence.

‧ The recent philosophy, "If it feels good, do it," is just as useless to the soul as repression. Extreme repression and extreme expression are both evidence of people who aren't going to grow up. They aren't going to learn very much from their experience. We are called to live in the middle, where you live with the energy for a while, the temptation, the experience, the moment, and you let it teach you even at the cost of pain. Repression is the means of control, expression is the means of avoiding control. Truth lies somewhere in between—the rightly-called "golden mean" or *via media*.

In that in-between place, we've got to build a bridge between power and powerlessness. Jesus taught us that we start on the side of powerlessness, but that doesn't make power wrong. Ultimately, we have to learn how to use power creatively. One word for the Holy Spirit is *dynamos*, which means "power." The only people who can be trusted with power are those who know how to live creatively with powerlessness. Liberals tend to hate or mistrust power. Conservatives tend to fear or avoid powerlessness.

The only people whom I can trust with saying "It's important to be Catholic," for example, are those who know that Catholic isn't finally what it's all about. The Kingdom is what it's all about! Once you are committed to Kingdom values, you can rightly pull back into a *healthy* exclusivity. We need a solid ground, an Archimedian point, from which we can move the world. I don't suppose there is any other way—at least I don't know of any historically. But it is a marvelous balancing act, a balancing act that few will take responsibility for today. Jesus seems to have achieved the human patience, the unwillingness to hurt or react, the critical intelligence and the urgent love that come together to create that rare thing called wisdom.

Transforming Initiatives

After the prefatory remarks that challenge both ends of the ideological spectrum (Matthew 5:17-20), Jesus now moves into his concrete analysis of the Mosaic Law. This reinterpretation has been written off by most of the Church as high-minded idealism. We don't really take it seriously because in our world order it is not realistic. If you took it seriously at all, you would be encouraged to interpret it in terms of private morality but not in terms of an institution, a group, a family—certainly not our nation-states! States can't possibly be encouraged to love their enemies or we'd have no world order, right?

Yet a scholar named Glen Stassen, points out in *Just Peacemaking* (Louisville, Ky.: Westminster/John Knox Press, 1992) that what we have here, beginning at Matthew 5:21, is not simply high-minded idealism but a concrete plan for deliverance from vicious cycles in fourteen verses. Each paragraph first states traditional piety, conventional religion, then what Stassen calls the mechanism of bondage or vicious cycle. Jesus' insight is that each good law—obeyed *apart from the Spirit*—carries with it a way to entrap you! (Isn't that exactly what Paul concludes in both Romans and Galatians?) After naming the mechanism of bondage, Jesus names the flip side, a transforming initiative. The term *triad*—a name for a musical chord of three interrelated tones—captures the unity of these three elements in each passage (see the following chart). This is the most helpful analysis of this section I have ever studied. It does not paralyze with idealism and force us to dismissal, nor does it back off from a very real initiative that we can take.

The Fourteen Triads of the Sermon on the Mount
Matthew 5:20—7:11

	Traditional challenge of a religious culture	But, the problem is:	The Way of Transformation
1	You shall not kill.	You still nurse anger and accusation.	Go, be reconciled first.
2	You shall not commit adultery.	Fantasy and lustful looking continue.	Way of seeing demands radical surgery.
3	Men may divorce by writ of dismissal.	This is one-sided adultery.	(Call to equality in dialogue seems to have been forgotten.)
4	Do not take oaths.	Legal swearing only binds you into loyalty systems and mistrust.	Keep your language very simple and personal.
5	"Eye for eye" morality as justice.	De facto vengeance and violent resistance.	You, change the rules of the game: "turn cheek," etc.
6	Love "family" and ignore/"hate" others.	This gets us nowhere and keeps our love small.	Love the outsider and practice by praying for them.

Traditional challenge of a religious culture	But, the problem is:	The Way of Transformation
Re-emphasized by: *Show recognition to those like you*	*Everybody does that:* *not really love or virtue.*	*GOD IMITATION:* *total inclusivity.*
7 Give alms to the poor.	Keeps religion on level of externals and observance. Maintains your morally superior image.	Do it secretly to avoid any public or personal payoff.
8 Pray.	Be wary of the perks of social prayer.	Contemplative prayer of quiet: behind door and no payoff.
9 More and better prayer will talk God into it.	This maintains you in a false relationship and image of God.	OUR FATHER names the relationship and world rightly.
10 Fast (necessary call to understimulation, detachment, simplifying).	Dour, dismal and overly serious religious people.	Keep it light, happy and smiling; do it for truth, not payoff.
11 Don't consume and hoard.	Greed never satisfies, and you lose it anyway.	Spiritual investment lasts. Do it!
12 Can't serve both God and the system ("Mammon.").	You still remain divided and enslaved and preoccupied.	It's not about the "hot sins" but anxiety about the daily things. "Stop worrying" repeated five times!
13 Do not judge.	Because it becomes the whole way you see reality and even yourself. Gives one a false sense of control and not truth or love.	Shadow denial leads to shadow projection. See yourself in others and *forgive it over there* to stop the cycle.
14 "Don't throw pearls before swine," etc.	Unready people only misunderstand and turn against you.	Ask, search, know, pray, wait. God will give "good things" in time.

Let's go through the triads briefly:

1   You have heard how it was said to our ancestors, *You shall not kill;* and if anyone does kill he must answer for it before the court. But I say this to you, anyone who is angry with a brother will answer for it before the court; anyone who calls a brother "Fool" will answer for it before the Sanhedrin; and anyone who calls him "Traitor" will answer for it in hell fire. So then, if you are bringing your offering to the altar and there remember that your brother has something against you, leave your offering there before the altar, go and be reconciled with your brother first, and then come back and present your offering. Come to terms with your opponent in good time while you are still on the way to the court with him, or he may hand you over to the judge and the judge to the officer, and you will be thrown into prison. In truth I tell you, you will not get out until you have paid the last penny. (Matthew 5:21-26)

The first sentence of this initiative is traditional religion. Who would disagree with it? But nursing anger is the mechanism of bondage. To nurse anger, for example, to call another person a fool and hold ill will against that person is going to get you just as trapped as killing and will finally lead you to killing. Therefore the transforming initiative: Go and be reconciled while there's still time, before you can nurse anger in your heart and build up hatred toward another person.

2   You have heard how it was said, *You shall not commit adultery.* But I say this to you, if a man looks at a woman lustfully, he has already committed adultery with her in his heart. If your right eye should be your downfall, tear it out and throw it away; for it will do you less harm to lose one part of yourself than to have your whole body thrown into hell. And if your right hand should be your downfall, cut it off and throw it away; for it will do you less harm to lose one part of yourself than to have your whole body go to hell. (Matthew 5:27-30)

Of course we must not commit adultery, but Jesus goes always one step deeper. The real mechanism of bondage is to look at another person as an object (with lust, as it says in the text). To commit adultery in the heart, to try to make another person an object for your consumption: That's the mechanism of bondage.

What is Jesus' transforming initiative? Remove even the cause of the temptation. Stop playing the whole mind-game called fantasy. His teaching images of tearing out eyes are an indication of how hard he knew it would be to discipline mind, heart and senses. It has nothing to do with the real world of relationship. That's the real sin: creating relationships in your head. Relationships don't happen in the head, they happen in the real world order. See how radical Jesus is: he always deals with causes, not symptoms. (A radical is one who gets to the *radix*, the root of things. That's neither a bad idea nor a negative criticism.)

3 It has also been said, *Anyone who divorces his wife must give her a writ of dismissal.* But I say this to you, everyone who divorces his wife, except for the case of an illicit marriage, makes her an adulteress; and anyone who marries a divorced woman commits adultery.
(Matthew 5:31-32)

The primary point of Jesus' teaching on divorce is to bring back equality between men and women, not to declare eternal indissolubility (the latter interpretation is a good example of how sexism kept us from reading the exact meaning of the text). Divorce was allowed in Jewish culture but totally from the side of the male. He had all the power. If he didn't like his wife's looks, one day he could declare that they were divorced. What Jesus is doing, again, is taking the oppressed side, the side of the feminine, and saying, "You men can't keep having it your way." It's an equal system and *both parties* must have the right to take the initiative. Justice and truth must be done between you, and *both* must take responsibility for the death of a marriage, which 5:32 seems to recognize will sometimes happen.

The mechanism of bondage is precisely one-sidedness from the male which destroys any real meaning of possible reconciliation, dialogue or basic justice. The transforming initiative is to create a *true partnership* and work from there. That's revolutionary teaching!

4 Again, you have heard how it was said to our ancestors, *You must not break your oath, but must fulfill your oaths to the Lord.* But I say this to you, do not swear at all, either by *heaven,* since that is *God's throne;* or by *earth,* since that is *his* footstool; or by Jerusalem, since that is *the city of the great King.* Do not swear by your own head either, since you cannot turn a single hair white or black. All you need say is "Yes" if you mean yes, "No" if you mean no; anything more than this comes from the Evil One. (Matthew 5:33-37)

The mechanism of bondage in this case is that swearing by anything involves you with evil and with judgment. Remember, that the system up until the time of the feudal age held together by the taking of oaths (see Chapter Four). We don't understand it so much because we don't understand the patron/client world of another era.

This, by the way, is an example that some things are taken from the teaching of Jesus and made absolute commandments, while other things are completely ignored. We're going to get the last bit of blood out of Jesus' injunction about adultery. But the very next injunction on taking oaths has been, for the most part, ignored. Jesus says, Don't promise your loyalty to any system. But do you know a single Christian who was ever kicked out of a Church for taking an oath? There are only a few sects which take this seriously. It's strange that perhaps we would consider the Amish to be sectarian, when their interpretation of the ban on oath-taking is likely correct and consistent.

Let your yes be yes, and your no be no, is Jesus' transforming initiative. Can we live in such a world where we talk with absolute simple truth to one another and our word is good? Allow me to repeat an example I've used elsewhere: My father ran a gas station in western Kansas. He used to speak of the hard times around the Great Depression. Many people couldn't pay even for five gallons of gas. He'd always just say, "When you can pay it, pay it." To his memory, almost all of them finally paid. He said that once someone came back and gave him a ten-dollar bill for the gas ten years later.

Now I know we can't go back to such a world. I'm sure if you went to your local gas station and told them you'll pay them later they wouldn't give you gas. But Jesus is taking the initiative about a new world order, where people's word can mean something to one another.

A world of oaths, swearing and suing (as we have today) is founded on mistrust, impersonalism and lack of relationship. That is the old world order, and yet even we Christians expect truth and justice from it.

We go to Caesar for what Christ has already offered us—but what we didn't accept from him. Interestingly, Saint Francis, in his Rule for the Third Order, required that laypeople neither possess "lethal weapons" nor take oaths, "except for peace, for the Faith, under calumny and in bearing witness." Recent historians have credited the widely followed Rule with partial responsibility for the fall of the entire feudal system of nobility and serfdom! Without arms and oaths of loyalty it could not stand. Did Jesus not have the same intention for the yeast that he was offering to civilization in these seemingly innocuous admonitions?

5   You have heard how it was said: *Eye for eye and tooth for tooth.* But I say this to you: offer no resistance to the wicked. On the contrary, if anyone hits you on the right cheek, offer him the other as well; if someone wishes to go to law with you to get your tunic, let him have your cloak as well. And if anyone requires you to go one mile, go two miles with him. Give to anyone who asks you, and if anyone wants to borrow, do not turn away.
(Matthew 5:38-42)

The mechanism of bondage here is violent resistance. The whole problem is in the inner attitude. Jesus' great transforming initiative is, "Turn the other cheek: Let him have your clothes as well. Why even play the game? If he asks you to go one mile with him, go two with him." In Jesus' time, a conscripted soldier was allowed to ask any person to carry his armor for one mile. That's the image Jesus is building on. He's saying, "Just don't get into the tit-for-tat game; carry it two. Create your own loving set of rules, which will blow the system apart. *You* take the initiative and change the rules, the expectations and the outcome."

6   You have heard how it was said: *You will love your neighbor* and hate your enemy. But I say this to you, love

your enemies and pray for those who persecute you; so that
you may be children of your Father in heaven, for he
causes his sun to rise on the bad as well as the good, and
sends down rain to fall on upright and the wicked alike.
For if you love those who love you, what reward will you
get? Do not even the tax collectors do as much? (Matthew
5:43-47)

Traditional piety says to love your neighbor, love the in-group.
Loving and greeting only those who love you, Jesus says, is simply
a mechanism of bondage. It's keeping you in a small world of warm
fuzzies, but actually inoculating you from the often dark and daring
world of real love. It actually protects and perpetuates the world of
scapegoats, victimization and projection.

This sixth triad is considered the most radical, demanding and
truthful of all of Jesus' teaching. Until there is love for enemies,
there is no real transformation, because the enemy always carries
the dark side of your own soul. Normally those people who threaten
us carry our own faults in a different form. The people who really
turn you off are very much like you. Jesus offers not just a
suggestion; you've *got* to love your enemy to grow up. Jesus rightly
puts it in the imperative form: *Do* it!

Also, what we don't like about ourselves is our inner enemy, in
a certain sense. We must learn to love and forgive that enemy, too.
Sometimes that takes great humility and great compassion, but if
we learn it internally, we will be prepared for the outer enemies.

And if you save your greetings for your brothers, are you
doing anything exceptional? Do not even the gentiles do as
much? You must therefore set no bounds to your love, just
as your heavenly Father sets none to his. (Matthew 5:47)

This sixth triad is one long but dramatic verse: If you greet only
your brother, what's so great about that? The ultimately alienating
process is that if we stay inside our religious/ethnic group, wars and
racism continue. That's just staying inside a kind of magnified
self-love. The key is always to love the stranger at the gate. Love
the one outside of your comfort zone, the outsider, the other. Until
you can enter into the outsider and the other, Jesus says, you really
have not loved at all. What's his motivation for doing this? The

all-inclusiveness of the Father.

What Jesus suggests is a kind of *imitatio Deo*, an imitation of God. If that's who God is and that's the way God loves, then that's how we want to love. God rubs off on people who hang around God. If God "sets no bounds," then we have to stop keeping score and weighing worthiness.

The final imperative is well translated here by the *New Jerusalem Bible*. The common translation, "be perfect" (*teleios*) is a later abstract, Greek concept which Jesus would never have used. He spoke in concrete and descriptive Aramaic metaphors, never like a cerebral philosopher or even a theologian. He is, however, admitting that this most demanding commandment is going to ask a great deal of us—boundlessness and magnanimity.

7   So when you give alms, do not have it trumpeted before you; this is what the hypocrites do in the synagogues and in the streets to win human admiration. In truth I tell you, they have had their reward. But when you give alms, your left hand should not know what your right is doing; your almsgiving must be secret, and your Father who sees all that is done in secret will reward you. (Matthew 6:2-4)

Giving alms is traditional piety. The mechanism of bondage is doing religious practices in public and getting hung up on what people think about you. Religion's perennial temptation is to get "trapped *in persona*." Externalization is always the avoidance of true relationship and communion. The transforming initiative: Don't do it out loud, do it secretly.

Remember what we said in Chapter Four about an honor/ shame culture. Jesus is trying to get his people to own their identity and motivation from within. He is trying to get them out of the hall of mirrors, the world of imitation and spiritual competition which keeps people shallow and essentially insecure. Don't let your left hand know what your right hand is doing—just *act* and forget about the rewards or fruits of your action. Act for the truth of the action itself and not for human approval or the flattering self-image. That is radical surgery.

8   And when you pray, do not imitate the hypocrites: they love to say their prayers standing up in the synagogues and

at the street corners for people to see them. In truth I tell
you, they have had their reward. But when you pray, *go to
your private* room, shut yourself in, and so pray to your
Father who is in that secret place, and your Father who
sees all that is done in secret will reward you.
(Matthew 6:5-6)

The mechanism of bondage is doing it in public; therefore, pray in
secret. In today's terms, go in the closet, where you have no
motivation except seeking the truth, seeking God, seeking love.
Again, Jesus wants action for its own sake and not for some outer
image or inner product.

This teaching is useful in contemplative training and for those
who say Jesus never taught contemplation. In his Semitic, concrete
style, he does speak of separation, quiet and under-stimulation with
the image of a closed closet door. He could also be interpreted as
advising a prayer style that does not seem to have any immediate or
social payoff. That's exactly what perseverance in contemplative
prayer requires. We sometimes forget that Jesus was a mystic.

9   In your prayers do not babble as the gentiles do, for they
think that by using many words they will make themselves
heard. Do not be like them; your Father knows what you
need before you ask him. So you should pray like this:
    Our Father in heaven
    may your name be held holy,
    your kingdom come,
    your will be done,
    on earth as in heaven.
    Give us today our daily bread.
    And forgive us our debts,
    as we have forgiven those who are in debt to us.
    And do not put us to the test,
    but save us from the Evil One.
Yes, if you forgive others their failings, your heavenly
Father will forgive you yours; but if you do not forgive
others, your Father will not forgive your failings either.
(Matthew 6:7-15)

A lot of us pray as if prayer is really twisting the arm of God or
convincing God to do something. We think by saying more words

we'll talk God into it. We think, "If I say it one more time, God will agree with me." That very attitude is an alienating attitude. It keeps us in the role of doing it "right" or often enough to convince an unready or unwilling God. Wrong, wrong, wrong!

Instead, Jesus gives us seven simple statements of petition to *align* our prayer with the eternal and effective will of God (as opposed to placating an angry God or talking God into things God would rather not do). This is Jesus' transforming initiative, an alternative to "babbling like the pagans." With an imperative, he says, "Pray like this," and presents the ideal spoken prayer.

10 When you are fasting, do not put on a gloomy look as the hypocrites do: they go about looking unsightly to let people know they are fasting. In truth I tell you, they have had their reward. But when you fast, put scent on your head and wash your face, so that no one will know you are fasting except your Father who sees all that is done in secret; and your Father who sees all that is done in secret will reward you. (Matthew 6:16-18)

Along with the traditional piety of fasting comes a mechanism of bondage: walking around revealing the self as fasting and observant. The transforming initiative: Anoint your head, wash your face, forget about any public display of fasting. It has to be done quietly within your own life and heart. Jesus is a master at breaking all "social contagion" which keeps humans interactive but utterly *ungrounded*. A certain degree of solitude and silence is the transforming mechanism in all three religious disciplines: prayer, almsgiving and fasting. Prayer frees us for God, almsgiving frees us for others and fasting frees us from ourselves.

11 Do not store up treasures for yourselves on earth, where moth and woodworm destroy them and thieves can break in and steal. But store up treasures for yourselves in heaven, where neither moth nor woodworm destroys them and thieves cannot break in and steal. For wherever your treasure is, there will your heart be too. (Matthew 6:19-21)

The alienating process is that consumerism finally lets you down anyway. It promises more than it can deliver. Get the lead on it by putting all your satisfaction somewhere else. Jesus uses the banking/investment image but instead applies it to spiritual goods. As John Paul II said to the United Nations, material goods decrease by usage, but spiritual goods actually increase when we make use of them. It's all a Semitic way of saying, "What you love reveals who you are."

12 No one can be the slave of two masters: he will either hate the first and love the second, or be attached to the first and despise the second. You cannot be the slave both of God and of money.

That is why I am telling you not to worry about your life and what you are to eat, nor about your body and what you are to wear. Surely life is more than food, and the body more than clothing! Look at the birds in the sky. They do not sow or reap or gather into barns; yet your heavenly Father feeds them. Are you not worth much more than they are? Can any of you, however much you worry, add one single cubit to your span of life? And why worry about clothing? Think of the flowers growing in the fields; they never have to work or spin; yet I assure you that not even Solomon in all his royal robes was clothed like one of these. Now if that is how God clothes the wild flowers growing in the field which are there today and thrown into the furnace tomorrow, will he not much more look after you, you who have so little faith? So do not worry; do not say, "What are we to eat? What are we to drink? What are we to wear?" It is the gentiles who set their hearts on all these things. Your heavenly Father knows you need them all. Set your hearts on his kingdom first, and on God's saving justice, and all these other things will be given you as well. So do not worry about tomorrow: tomorrow will take care of itself. Each day has enough trouble of its own. (Matthew 6:24-34)

This oft-quoted passage speaks better than any commentary, but to illustrate the triad as Matthew carries it out: (1) The traditional religious practice is to have it both ways, love the system and still love God. (2) Jesus says it will prove impossible, that it will hold you bound. (3) The transforming initiative is not to be anxious (repeated in five ways) and, positively, to "set your heart on God's kingdom and God's justice." That's classic Jesus teaching in summary and poetic form.

13   Do not judge, and you will not be judged; because the
judgments you give are the judgments you will get, and the
standard you use will be the standard used for you. Why do
you observe the splinter in your brother's eye and never
notice the great log in your own? And how dare you say to
your brother, "Let me take that splinter out of your eye,"
when, look, there is a great log in your own? Hypocrite!
Take the log out of your own eye first, and then you will
see clearly enough to take the splinter out of your brother's
eye. (Matthew 7:1-5)

Why do you think Jesus tells us not to judge? First of all, judgment
is very often a means of control, not a means of looking for the
truth. It's a means of securing the self or undoing other people by
categorizing them. Sometimes we hate and condemn ourselves in
the same way. That type of judgment is not of God. Judging a
person to be morally superior or morally inferior, right or wrong,
good or bad seldom leads to deeper insight or compassion. It's
another way of eating of the tree of knowledge of good and evil and
gaining a false sense of security or moral high ground.

Yet there's another form of judgment that is absolutely
necessary: choosing for ourselves between two options. This is a
value, this is not a value; this is what God is calling me to, this is
not what God is calling me to. Call it discrimination or
discernment, if you will. It is not only good, but a necessary and
holy meaning of our English word *judgment*.

Because *judgment* in English has these two meanings, this has
been a problematic passage for many people. You say, well, we've
got to make judgments. True, but whenever you're doing it to
control or to condemn yourself or others, to explain or to justify or
to validate yourself or others, at that point you're not normally
looking for truth, you're looking for control. That's the judgment
Jesus is talking about in this passage. It's a form of entrapment to
be avoided. Now we know that Jesus was a student of human nature
far ahead of his times. This particular passage is an excellent
statement on self-hatred, denial of shadow and necessary projection
of denied shadow. Psychologist Carl Jung even referred to Jesus'

excellent and transforming initiative: "Take the log out of your own eye" means the same as "own your own shadow."

14   Do not give dogs what is holy; and do not throw your pearls in front of pigs, or they may trample them and then turn on you and tear you to pieces.
     Ask, and it will be given to you; search, and you will find; knock, and the door will be opened to you. Everyone who asks receives; everyone who searches finds; everyone who knocks will have the door opened. Is there anyone among you who would hand his son a stone when he asked for bread? Or would hand him a snake when he asked for a fish? If you, then, evil as you are, know how to give your children what is good, how much more will your Father in heaven give good things to those who ask him! (Matthew 7:6-11)

There's no point in giving wisdom or truth to people who psychically, spiritually aren't ready for it. That may seem like a harsh statement to us but it's utter realism. Sometimes when you offer truth too early, people write off the whole thing because the heart or soul isn't ready for it yet. Then they are worse off than when you started.

I saw many people, for example, naively come to join communities in the early 70's, when the community movement was strong. They really weren't coming for the right reasons. There was no real discernment. They were often avoiding home or wanting a belonging system. Their souls weren't ready for it. They were given a pearl of great price and truth but they had no capacity for such truth. Many of these folks left community and now they speak despairingly of the "c-word." Often one feels that pearls "were trampled on" by the very people who received the most, and moreover "they turned on you and tore you to pieces." Jesus sounds like he is speaking from experience.

Jesus understands timing, patience and growth. His transforming initiative is to give the request to God in prayer: "Ask, and it will be given to you; search and you will find; knock, and the door will be opened to you" (Matthew 7:7). In other words, hold off, don't push the river. Don't demand blood from a turnip. Ask, search, knock. He moves the temptation to anger, blame and self-pity to an entirely different framework. Don't waste time with shame and blame. Seek "good things"—bread, fish and open doors—from a God who is apparently the Ultimate Parent.

When you wait, when you listen, when you "knock and ask," you find out the real demons, the sources of bondage, the real things that are tying you up. They're usually not what they seem. A lot of anger today is grief, I'm convinced. Some of today's fear is grief, too.

Yet you can't build on fear *or* anger. You can't build in the negative. You only can build on faith, on freedom, on truth. If you build on fear, in the end you will have a house of fear. To build on anger is not to build at all, for the anger will return to you in your children, your employees and your own sour soul.

Many people derive lots of energy today being angry at the pope, bishops, priests, husbands, wives, or whomever else. In the end, it's a waste of time. Nothing is built. Jesus ends the Sermon on the Mount contrasting the one who built a house on rock to the one who built on sand (see Matthew 7:24-27).

I never thought any of my words would be on a T-shirt, but when I handed over the Center for Action and Contemplation in Albuquerque to lay leadership, they printed shirts. Of all my too-many words they chose these for the back: "You cannot build on death, you can only build on life. We must be sustained by a sense of what we are for and not just what we are against." That was the end of my sermon too, I guess.

The Lord's Prayer

Now let us go back into the Sermon and give special treatment to the Our Father, the Lord's Prayer, the prayer that Jesus taught us. Books, of course, have been written on it. But perhaps in a few pages we can glean some insights. When I was in hermitage a few years ago, I spent a lot of time trying not only to study it but also to pray it and understand it on a deeper level. This is what stayed with me:

First, the prayer aligns all relationships truthfully and situates us correctly in the universe if we just believe it and act out of it. Beginning with the first word, *our*, we are taught that we are social beings and that our relationship with God is not "mine" or private. We either come to God together or we don't come.

Second, a healthy sense of spirituality is a sense that God is simultaneously *transcendent* and *immanent*. It senses a God who dwells within—each of us is a temple of the Holy Spirit—but equally a God who is utterly beyond, whom you and I can only bow down before. The very first phrase of the Lord's Prayer keeps that perfectly in balance.

"Our Father in heaven" (Matthew 6:9b): God is the beloved *Abba*, the beloved parent who dwells within each of us and in whose image we are created. Yet this loving God who does not accuse us, who does not shame us but, in fact, nurtures us and holds us, is also totally beyond us *"in heaven."* Contemporary spirituality and practice still seek that ideal synthesis. Most groups exaggerate one side or the other. Jesus names both true.

"[M]ay your name be held holy" (Matthew 6:9c): Great religion is about adoration, about Someone you bow before. If you do not, you will soon bow before yourself. If the center of the world is not out there, there's only one other place it will reside and that's in your own limited self. You will be egocentric. Human beings *must* worship. Saint Francis says everything that exists is to be adored because God created it. So Francis is in love with the God out there while perfectly at home with the God shining through material creation.

This phrase of the Lord's Prayer is also saying that God is not nameable. The First and Second Commandments say that whatever word you use for God will be a metaphor (see Exodus 20:4-7). Don't use the name of God in vain, don't use it lightly or easily because it will never be adequate. So keep the name holy. Use it delicately and with humility. The Hebrews didn't speak it at all because they knew whatever they spoke would be wrong. We would be much wiser had we learned some of that.

In some Hindu temples you walk through several courts and the inner court is absolutely empty. I saw the same in some Zen Buddhist temples in Japan, except with a twist: When you finally get to the inner court there is simply a mirror. Both the Hindus and the Buddhists have a marvelous truth. When you finally get to the center there's no name. You simply stand in the middle of the

mystery. The middle court of the temple is usually dark, too. *Holy*
(*Kadosh*) literally means separate, beyond, too much—or as our
youth would say, "far out."

"[Y]our kingdom come,/your will be done/on earth, as in
heaven" (Matthew 6:10): By saying, "your Kingdom come," we're
inviting it into this world, Jesus says. We invite the eternal truth to
happen now in our midst on earth, as in heaven. That is the bridging
of the great schism. What it means to live in the Kingdom is to live
the final state of affairs now. The first three petitions are for God's
dominion in history and over us—a theocentric prayer that
correctly realigns the order and keeps us out of the center.

If the first three petitions situate us correctly within the
universe, the following four situate us as free people inside our own
history: free to need God, to need one another and to rely upon
God's protection. Most people would consider that a freedom.

"Give us today our daily bread./And forgive us our debts,/as we
have forgiven those who are in debt to us" (Matthew 6:12): These
phrases on bread and debts are clearly a prayer given to the poor.
Bread and debt are the preoccupation, the entire life, of the peasant
class. How do I have food for tomorrow and how do I pay my bills?
In old English the word was rendered as *trespasses*, which seems
unchangeable now because we've said it for so long. But have no
doubt about it, the word in the original text is clearly an economic
word. Several of today's most respected New Testament
translations reflect that (*New Jerusalem* and *New Revised Standard*
Version, for example).

We have spiritualized this petition, as we did most of the
gospel. We made this petition refer to private, individual
forgiveness, you trespassing against me. And surely it does have
that meaning. But on the first level this petition really refers to
economic indebtedness. The power of this petition lies in the
jubilee year, described in Leviticus 25:8-17. That's what Jesus is
drawing upon. In ancient Israel, in every fiftieth year everything
went back to its original owner (see page 132). Ideally, all debts
were forgiven. It was the great equalizer. It was a sign of the largess
and magnanimity of God.

If people had lived by the law of jubilee, Communism would
never have been necessary and capitalism would have never been

possible. The spirit behind this jubilee thinking lasted for the first 1000 years of Christianity, when one could be excommunicated for taking an interest on a loan (usury). The petition still raises questions about economics: How does the burden of debt—the personal debt people carry in our consumer society, the national debt carried particularly by Third World countries—keep people imprisoned in their own history?

Because of the economic meaning, 6:14-15, the warning to forgive others if we expect God to forgive us, was probably added to deal with personal sinfulness and forgiveness.

Asking for our daily bread is simply to trust that each day will take care of itself. What do the Twelve-Step people say? One day at a time. That's what Jesus is saying here, too. Don't live an anxious life of preparation for tomorrow.

In speaking of bread, Jesus is also building on the tradition of the manna. During the Exodus, the manna in the desert was only enough for the day. If they collected more than one day's worth it would rot (see Exodus 16:4, 19-21). There's the symbolism: What you store up will rot. Living for today keeps us interdependent. *Daily* might be translated as "just enough," so we need God and one another to get through our days. That is surely on a course directly opposite from our culture, which prides itself on independence, self-sufficiency, personal control and now shopping "home alone" by TV or computer.

"And do not put us to the test, but deliver us from the Evil One" (Matthew 6:13): Our way of saying the same, perhaps, would be: "Make it easy for us, God. We are relying upon you because we can't do it by ourselves." Although this line is bothersome to many people because it seems to imply that God deliberately tests us, I think Jesus asked *us* to say it to realign ourselves with *what we need to trust*—that God will never lead us where his love cannot sustain us. That is a great relief for anyone who has ever been led to the edge.

"Yes, if you forgive others their failings, your heavenly Father will forgive you yours; but if you do not forgive others, your Father will not forgive your failings either" (Matthew 6:14-15): In case the disciples rejected the point about debts and the economic order, now, in the final verse, Jesus does move it to the private order. It's

the only petition that's repeated so you can't possibly miss the issue of forgiveness. I believe forgiveness is the whole gospel: beginning, middle and end.

The fourteen triads are then summed up in a transformative one-liner that perhaps sums up their entire momentum. No wonder we call it "the golden rule": "[A]lways treat others as you would like them to treat you; that is the Law and the Prophets" (Matthew 7:12).

Either/Or Language From a Both/And God

Like any good spiritual teacher, Jesus sums up his sermon by calling his listeners to a choice, or an "altar call" as the tent meetings would describe it. The options are set before us in very clear and decisive fashion. Do you want the old world order, or do you want the new one that I have just described? In a few verses he will describe two roads, two kinds of prophecy, two kinds of disciples and two kinds of houses. There is no room for any in-between in Matthew's formulation of the Sermon.

Decisiveness is clearly seen as crucial to faith. Unless there is an organizing principle, unless one is Lord, we will be lost in our own small world of preferences, interpretations and cultural moods. We have no choice, it seems. We must place our bet. We must surrender to Another, or we will be subject to ourselves.

Russian philosopher Nicholas Berdyaev put it very well: "Inner division wears away the personality and this division can be overcome only by making a choice—by selecting a definite object for one's love." That definite object is, for us, the Reign of God and the person of Jesus.

Jesus describes the two roads as either "wide," leading to destruction, or "narrow" and "hard" that lead to life. Many take the first, he says, and few find the second (see Matthew 7:13-14). The wide road that is taken is clearly a graphic description of what we would later call groupthink, mimetic consciousness, mob psychology—the ordinary and predictable paths of religious, economic and political cultures. Left to ourselves, that is what we will likely do.

The narrow road that is found is our new world order. Jesus has just described it for us and encourages us to take "the road less traveled." It is interesting that a book by that name holds the record for being the all-time best-seller (after the Bible)—almost as if we know the common path is not it.

The two kinds of prophets or truth-speakers are to be discerned by one criterion—the kind of "fruit" that their lives create. Not, mind you, by their mild manner ("sheep's clothing") or even their claims about themselves ("a sound tree") but by what is its final effect.

The old world order is built on a lie about the nature of reality. It allows us to use, exploit and even destroy the divine image in other creatures. Any system which allows or even encourages you to objectify God's creatures for your own purposes is evil and will always produce evil fruit. Of course, this can never be seen from inside the system. Economic progress looks like progress when you are totally inside an economic culture. Listen to our people and our politicians as they accept this unthinkingly. Mere economic progress is bad fruit only from the measuring line of the Reign of God. If you are blinded from inside, you will never see it. Thus this simple criterion of "judge by the fruits" never felt very helpful to most people, and it isn't, unless you have already been blown away by the preceding sermon. If so, you know exactly what fruit Jesus is talking about.

The two kinds of disciples are also very telling. Jesus does not describe any ideal kind of creed or cult—but only a code of conduct. Jesus' emphasis is clearly on what we call "orthopraxy" (correct behavior or practice) over any kind of orthodoxy (correct thinking or opinion). To make this point he even risks "offending pious ears," as we used to say: "It is not anyone who says to me, 'Lord, Lord,' who will enter the kingdom of Heaven, but the person who does the will of my Father in heaven" (Matthew 7:21) that matters.

We in the Church traditions had better meditate on those lines for a long time. Why have we burned people at the stake for what they thought but hardly ever for what they did (unless it was an affront to churchly power)? Or better, why did we ever burn anybody at the stake at all?! Something got very mixed up here. It was still the old world order, hiding behind the glory of the new world order, and creating victims as it always does. The old world order "was a murderer from the start;/[it] was never grounded in the truth.... [it] is a li[e], and the father of lies" (John 8:44).

John's later description of Satan as the deceiver and murderer fits Matthew's understanding of the false way, the false teacher and the false disciple. You can tell them all by their fruits—they will always be looking for victims to blame, exclude and even kill. It is the litmus test of whether one truly has the Spirit of God. Jesus, and his true disciples, have no need or desire to create victims. Jesus and his true disciples will not lie about God. God is good, and that good image is to be recognized and honored in all living things. It really is that simple. The old world order cannot accept such simplicity. The new world order can see nothing else.

These two "houses" are described as built either on sand or on rock (Matthew 7:24-27). Those who "listen" and "build" will not fall. Those who "listen" but "do not act on them" will be "stupid." They will fall, "and what a fall they will have."

Finally, Jesus signs the document, after such a rousing conclusion, by describing himself in a most unique way. There are two kinds of authority too: one, "like the scribes and Pharisees" (see Matthew 7:28), needs to prop itself up by a reference or footnote to past religious authority or tradition, whereas Jesus' "teaching made a deep impression on the people because he taught with [inherent] authority." He taught with a nonacademic, layman's street wisdom, as we would say. It just rang true. It felt true. It was true, not because any authority said so, but because the Spirit confirmed it in the hearts of mature listeners. It is the same today.

The Foundation for the New World Order

In conclusion, allow me to give a simplified summary of what seems to be Jesus' foundational worldview and plan:

1) God is a God who can be trusted. God is like a loving "Father" who is involved in our lives and our world. So do not be afraid.

2) This God alone has the power to effect lasting and real change. Alignment with such truth is to live under the "Reign of God."

3) We are transformed to this Reign of God through a purifying journey into powerlessness and back. Jesus talked about it, then walked it through, and invited us to walk his Paschal Mystery ourselves.

4) Power unrefined by this journey into powerlessness will always be destructive and self-serving. It is unworthy of our loyalty or our hope. Therefore we must:

- Refuse our total allegiance ("idolatry") to all human systems of power, while still working around and even with them in a life of right relationship and service for justice.
- Refuse to idolize or idealize the private self, which props itself up by myths of importance, control and wealth.
- Offer ourselves trustfully to a much larger pattern, because *our lives are not about us!*

5) The motivation for all morality and religion is the imitation of God, who is love. When religion bases itself in fear, duty, honor, a need for law and order, a need for a superior self-image or group cohesiveness, it is corrupt. It looks good and will have many defenders, but is actually at the heart of the problem. The real God is no longer needed or even wanted and such religion usually becomes the actual enemy of God. The crucifixion of Jesus speaks to this.

6) This new world order, where love and power now work together, is seen by Jesus as a "wedding banquet." Meals seem to be his most constant image of what it is all about. Jesus seems to imply a world that is good, joy-filled, trustworthy, relational, communal, shared, and somehow at the same time local and small-scale. Revolutionary on all points!

7) He teaches a "style of listening" and learning wisdom that emphasizes: (1) prayer of quiet and awareness, (2) social worship within a community and Tradition, (3) reliance upon the Holy Spirit for guidance, (4) a wisdom that "will draw out from its storehouse things both old and new," and (5) a life of service to the suffering world—which is to imitate God.

Epilogue

F riedrich Nietzsche, a German philosopher and critic who died at
the turn of the century, probably recognized the new world
order that Jesus was teaching better than the vast majority of
Christians. Unfortunately, he consciously chose against it. A genius
in many ways, he saw the direction and the final significance of the
Sermon on the Mount for human and European culture. He was
convinced that culture needed myths of power and "heroism" to
achieve what he saw as greatness. He said that the teachings of
Jesus would keep us like slaves and sheep.

Nietzsche rightly told his contemporaries that they were finally
going to have to choose between this Jesus (who had already
slowed them down) and the great mythic gods of Greece and
Germany, which we now see are the tribal gods of economic,
political and religious cultures. In this century many followed
Nietzsche's advice, with disastrous consequences.

The twentieth century has been a succession of waves, each
seeking dominance over the other, each seeing itself as the new and
only answer. These waves were playing out the patterns that had
already been given us by the Enlightenment, the French and
American Revolutions, and the Western philosophy of unlimited
progress. It became modernism, which told us we could do it all,
have it all and explain it all. When modernism appeared to fail,
especially after the wars and holocausts of Christian nations, we
fell into the present hopelessness called post-modernism. If reason,
science, education and technology cannot save us, then maybe there
is no salvation. Maybe there are no universal patterns that are
always true, maybe there is no beginning, middle or end, maybe
there are only private moments of meaning that we can grab from
the universe. Even among many cultural Christians, the operative

religion seems to be an official skepticism. If there is no *Reign of God,* it is a disenchanted and absurd world that we must live in.

It is a time that feels like exile, in both our country and our Church. Cynicism comes easily, too easily. Cynicism takes no surrender, no trust, no love and no intelligence. It is no wonder so many of us hide there. It is too easy to dismiss whatever does not work *for us* and *right now,* especially if we think that our lives are about us.

Jesus has offered us a more spacious world, a world where I do not have to explain it, fix it or control it; a world where we can allow a larger Mystery to work itself out through us and in us; a world where relationship is the beginning, the middle and the end. It is, of course, still two worlds: the world as it is and the world as we now know it should be. One is founded in dominative power, and the other is a self-renewing call to right relationship. So many have tried, so many have given up, so many are pointing in other messianic directions. So many, even in the Church, seem to have chosen power over love. Why should we keep proclaiming this kingdom?!

All I know is that Jesus proclaimed the kingdom in a time of history when his people were occupied, discouraged and enslaved, when religion was often corrupt, and the numbers who understood were few. Yet he said, *the Kingdom of God is in your midst!* What is the alternative? Does anyone else have a greater wisdom or a greater vision? *To whom else shall we go?*

The more countries where I preach, the more I see human history grinding down to a glacial freeze of remembered hurts, past oppressions and family feuds that are held against one another unto the fourth and fifth generations. Now with better research and history, we have even more convincing reasons to resent one another! Everybody is a victim, everybody can prove that they were oppressed somewhere, everybody has a righteous grudge. Where do we find justice?

Unable to find *justification* in our minds or hearts, we go to courts of law, we seek vengeance and call it justice, we seek desperately for someone to blame because we are unhappy. Our unforgiveness leaves *us* prisoners as we guard the prison door of those we hate and fear. Even Christians seek from the Law what was only promised us in the Spirit. We go to Caesar's house because Christ's stable seems so insecure. We have no home.

Fortunately, "Wisdom has built herself a house " (Proverbs 9:1). To live in this house of Wisdom is to let go of the past—and allow a future. To live in this house is to shake the dust from our feet—and live in a truly new way, the way of justice and mercy. It is all about forgiveness. Nothing new happens without forgiveness: the unmerited, the unnecessary, the totally gratuitous inbreaking of God into our systems of logic and culture.

Isn't that what God would likely do? Isn't that what we need all desire? If this is not good news, *what* would be good news?

Other Works by Richard Rohr

Books

Radical Grace: Daily Meditations by Richard Rohr.
Edited by John Bookser Feister. B2570. $13.95

The Great Themes of Scripture: New Testament.
By Richard Rohr and Joseph Martos. B0985. $6.95

The Great Themes of Scripture: Old Testament.
By Richard Rohr and Joseph Martos. B0853. $7.95

The Wild Man's Journey: Reflections on Male Spirituality.
By Richard Rohr and Joseph Martos. B1280. $17.95

Why Be Catholic? Understanding Our Experience and Tradition.
By Richard Rohr and Joseph Martos. B1019. $6.95

Audiocassettes

A Man's Approach to God: Four Talks on Male Spirituality.
A2800. $29.95

Breathing Under Water: Spirituality and the 12 Steps. A0150.
$17.95

Fire From Heaven: A Retreat for Men. A6130. $64.95

Gravity and Grace: Insights Into Christian Ministry. A6451. $8.95

Letting Go: A Spirituality of Subtraction. A4200. $64.95

Preparing for Christmas With Richard Rohr. A5200. $17.95

*Rebuild the Church: Richard Rohr's Challenge for the New
Millennium.* A6280. $39.95

Why Be Catholic? A3350. $34.95

**To order, write St. Anthony Messenger Press, 1615 Republic
St., Cincinnati, OH 45210, or call toll-free 1-800-488-0488.**